BUYING A BOAT

BUYING A BOAT

Colin Jarman

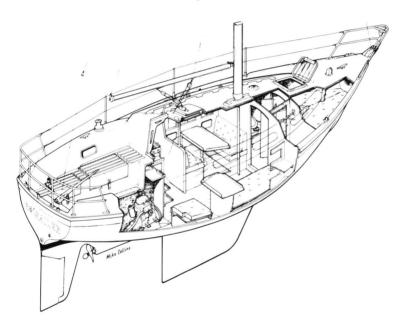

Mike Collins

DAVID & CHARLES
Newton Abbot   London

© Colin Jarman 1980

All photographs are by the Author except as follows:

Colvic Craft: pp 120, 122–3
Copland Boats: p 70 (bottom)
Mary Jarman: p 179
Motor Boat and Yachting (Eric Coltham) pp 115, 141, 163
Westerly Marine Construction: p 137
Yachting Monthly: p 29 (top right and bottom)

British Library Cataloguing in Publication Data

Jarman, Colin
  Buying a boat.
  1. Boats and boating
  I. Title
  623.82'02   GV777.6

ISBN 0–7153–7960–7

Photoset and printed in Great Britain by
Redwood Burn Limited
Trowbridge & Esher
for David & Charles (Publishers) Limited
Brunel House Newton Abbot Devon

CONTENTS

INTRODUCTION

For many people it is only a small step from sitting on some river bank or sea shore watching a variety of boats out sailing or seeing some athletic youth water-skiing to wanting a boat of their own. Despite financial strictures, the desire to get afloat can become, indeed does become, overwhelming and then all problems are swept aside in one grand decision—to buy a boat.

Even for those of us who have owned several boats and believe we know the ropes, buying each new one can become an emotional matter. We try to appear dispassionate, weighing all the pros and cons, doing various calculations about costs and insurance, but more often than not we end up with the boat that wins our hearts. Be that as it may we do need to go into the business with our eyes open so that when we eventually close them and open our cheque books there is some hope that we will actually have made a practical choice. The aim of this book is to help you, whether buying your first or your next boat, to think through the many aspects and to guide you towards that sensible, if still emotional, choice.

Colin Jarman
Burnham–on–Crouch
Summer 1980

1 THINKING IT ALL OUT

Buying a boat is not a matter for instant, unthinking action.
There are innumerable points to be considered and sorted out
before going ahead with the expenditure of what, for most of us,
is a rather large sum of money (which may take years to repay),
on an object that is likely to dominate our lives and may put the
fear of God into us between times of ecstatic happiness. Rushing
headlong into boating is as dangerous as trying to sell raffle
tickets to a lion tamer while he is at work. That is not to say
boating, in any of its many forms, is more dangerous than other
physically demanding sports, just that care and forethought are
required at all stages and at all times. Particularly forethought—
thinking ahead so that you are always ready to cope with a devel-
oping situation.

Forethought and planning begin with the kind of boating that
appeals to you. Do you want to take up dinghy sailing? Circuit
powerboat racing? Water-skiing? Family cruising under power
or sail? Offshore racing? The appeal of each of these facets of
boating is unique. No part of the general sport is quite like any
other.

The thrill of driving a small sportsboat at upwards of 40 knots
can only be likened to driving an open-topped car on an empty
motorway. In smooth water it is sheer exhilaration; in choppy
waters it can be a spine-jarring purgatory. It appeals to many
though and circuit racing with powerboat clubs is increasingly
popular, but the majority of sportsboats are bought to tow water-
skiers.

Dinghy sailing is often considered *the* way to learn how to sail

9

and admittedly it does sharpen up your reflexes—otherwise you go swimming as the boat capsizes—but I would suggest that it may well be better for adults, particularly those who confess to middle age, to learn in either a dayboat with a good heavy keel or else a sailing cruiser. At any rate, something that is not going to capsize every few minutes if the crew makes a mistake or reacts a little slowly; a boat that is forgiving. Then, having learnt basic boat handling, if dinghy sailing still appeals, you are in a much better position to try it. You are still likely to capsize, and you must learn to cope with a capsize, but you will discover the pleasures of dinghy sailing more quickly. Then before you know it you will be joining in club races and local regattas, then travelling to open meetings, national championships, changing to an Olympic class . . . well, there's no harm in dreaming, is there?

Cruising with your family, whether in a motor cruiser or a sailing one, can either bring you all very close together, united by a shared enjoyment of being afloat and of the places visited, or it can produce a sharp division. There is no guaranteed way to make a success of family cruising, but it must largely come down to an ability on everyone's part to think about the other members of the family. It is not unusual for father and son to want to go charging off to foreign parts despite a forecast of strong headwinds, while mother and younger children want to visit the local museum. The decision about which to do must be tempered by the fact that it is supposed to be a family holiday and the certainty that once badly scared, people are going to be reluctant to go afloat again.

There is immense pleasure to be gained from making a passage to a new port, exploring it thoroughly and sailing on. It can also be refreshing and relaxing to lie at anchor in a quiet backwater watching the tide ebb and flow, counting stars and reading bedtime stories. Each may be a different pleasure, but they are still essential parts of cruising.

Then again, for many boat owners the pleasure lies not so much in going to sea or even wandering far from the home berth or mooring, but in working on the boat, keeping her smart and maintaining the engines for the time when they *might* be wanted. People have been known to take years over building a boat and then sell her after one season to start building another. Their boating fun is based on dry land, but they still feel a part of the boating experience.

The question of boating safety often arises, particularly when there has been some spectacular rescue by helicopter or lifeboat which has either been on TV or has had front page mention in the newspapers. At such times there are calls for restrictions and tighter controls, cries which ignore thousands of people's perfect safety record each season.

Much emphasis is put on safety at sea by instructional books and magazines, and rightly so, but it can be overdone. At a symposium on 'going foreign' not so long ago almost all the questions were on tactics for coping with gales and heavy weather. Only at the end was one woman brave enough to ask the panel if they couldn't tell her just what fun a foreign cruise could be and how smooth the sea is occasionally. She was right. Seagoing is fun for probably 80 per cent of the time, but it is that remaining 20 per cent that frightens or at least preoccupies so many people. The possibility of bad weather cannot be ignored, but it should be treated as a possibility rather than a probability, in just the same way as one allows for the possibility of the car breaking down on a journey but does not let it prevent one starting the journey.

Safety at sea is promoted by a combination of a sound boat and a sound crew. While a corked bottle will survive a storm, it cannot be controlled; it is at the mercy of the storm. A boat must be capable of direction and the crew must remain in control of her. They are then a basically safe seagoing unit.

What constitutes dangerous conditions varies from one type of boat to another and from the soundness of construction of one boat to another, apart from the strength or expertise of the crew. A rowing dinghy would be a most unsuitable craft to take out in open waters in a strong wind, but in the same wind a 30ft sailing cruiser may be at her best. On the other hand, if two boats, one professionally built of top-quality materials and the other

amateur constructed of sub-standard materials, were faced with the same testing conditions, it is likely that the poorly built one would be in trouble long before the sound boat, even if their crews were of equal ability.

Generally, however, it should be emphasized that boating is enjoyable. It does have to be taken seriously, but it is enjoyable. One of the most dangerous descriptions anyone has come up with is that of 'messing about in boats'. Don't mess about, stay safe and happy.

Your kind of boating

Before considering specific types of craft you must come to a decision about what kind of boating you are going to enjoy most. Initially this comes down to a choice between some form of motorboating and some kind of sailing. Which you choose is entirely a matter of personal taste, but it will affect both the kind of boat you buy and the area (or areas) in which you do your boating. For example, local bye-laws may prevent you water-skiing in an area where sailing is permitted and vice versa.

You also need to consider who will be going afloat with you; is this to be a family hobby or yours alone, or you and one member of the family, or what? After all, you can all cruise on a narrow-boat on the inland waterways, but you can't all get aboard a singlehanded sailing dinghy at the same time. Do you want to potter with the family or are you going to try offshore racing with some of the lads?

Daysailing in a keelboat or one with a good, heavy centreplate, may suit your family better than going for weekends on a small powerboat or sailing cruiser. You need to discuss it and think it all out.

The International Cadet class (see opposite and pages 14 and 15), sailed by children up to the age of 17, has produced many world-class helmsmen. Boats are handed on from one generation to the next with a fairly constant growth in numbers as top helmsmen have new boats built to help them maintain their position at the head of the fleet

If you have some distance to go to the water this must be taken into account. After all, a three or four hour drive each way, together with time for rigging, launching and recovering a boat might make daysailing impractical. In addition you need to work out how much time you will have available for boating and how much time you are prepared to devote to it. Once you have a cruiser and begin going away for weekends or longer, the grass at home grows faster, the house needs repainting more often and there are Pony Club events that daughters have to be taken to almost every week—or so it seems.

You may be hoping to join a local club and take part in their activities, in which case it is as well to look at what kind of boating is catered for and decide whether or not it will suit you. If the club races only one class of dinghy in any numbers and you prefer another then it may be as well to look for a different club. If you are interested in cruising and everyone else in the club races, you may end up using the clubhouse as a base but never talking to anyone, which is a pity. Also, if the kind of boating you are after is not carried out by other members of the local clubs you would be wise to ask why, since it is possible that some factor you are unaware of makes the area unsuitable for your kind of boat.

Available water may also determine the kind of boating you take up. If you live close to a good sailing river or estuary you are likely to be aware of what boating goes on there and can decide whether or not it suits you, but if you have some distance to travel to *any* water, you may be faced with a choice of sites offering different facilities. There may be a reservoir or flooded gravel pit within reach where there is a lot of dinghy sailing or waterskiing, or you may live within reach of the coast where all sorts of boating goes on, or there may be a canal not too far away. The possibilities are endless, but you must consider them all, even if you immediately reject one or two.

Moorings and storage

In most places today moorings are at a premium as all available places are being used and the creation of new marinas is both a slow and highly expensive business. Before you buy a boat which

is to be kept afloat you must look for a mooring, and it is possible that in the end, the kind of boat you buy will be one for which you can get a mooring rather than one which you initially set out to buy. Naturally the compromise should not be too great, but you may want a boat with a deep keel to keep in a marina and have to settle for one that can take the ground on a drying mooring.

It is because of this pressure on mooring space that the 'trailer sailer' is a fast-growing breed. These boats can be launched and recovered from a trailer, towed behind a family car and stored ashore, even in a garden, thus requiring no permanent mooring. They also allow their owners to trail them to different locations, adding interest and variety to a summer holiday. Small motor cruisers too can be moved about like this, but you do have to find suitable launching sites and that is not always easy.

A visit to local marinas, boatyards and clubs in the chosen boating area will reveal the mooring situation, and once you have a fairly clear idea of the boat you are likely to buy, it is as well to make a firm booking for a mooring or berth. This may sound like putting the cart before the horse, but which is worse; paying for an unused berth (which can always be re-let if you don't find the boat you want) for a short while, or having a boat and nowhere to put her? If you do this though you must be prepared to relinquish the mooring if you take too long finding the right boat as it is unfair to prevent someone else who needs a mooring from obtaining one.

Choice of mooring type also depends on what is available, but generally lies between a marina berth, a deepwater mooring or a drying one. In a marina you can walk aboard down a pontoon and there is usually electricity and water laid on to each berth, while a deep water mooring requires you to go out in a dinghy with all your gear and there is no electricity or water laid on. A drying mooring is like a deep water one but is only accessible at certain states of the tide. This may sound like the worst option, but it may be the cheapest and with the right kind of boat and a degree of organisation (to ensure you catch the tide) it can be perfectly acceptable. Otherwise, a marina berth is likely to be the most expensive and the most convenient for getting on and off the boat and for enjoying home comforts such as television and warm air heaters, while a deep water mooring falls somewhere in between. It may be a little inconvenient to reach, but you can stay a night on board without having to move from the mooring and without having a lot of other people too close at hand, possibly making more noise than you would like.

Canal cruisers are usually kept in marinas similar to those on tidal waters or else moored alongside the bank. The former is again likely to have water and electricity laid on while the latter offers some degree of seclusion.

As for dinghies and towable boats, either sail or power, the problem is one of land-storage space. Most dinghy sailing clubs have their own boat parks, but trailer sailers and small motorboats must either be taken home each time or kept at a boatyard.

All these things need investigation and must be worked out while you are still at the considering stage rather than after you have taken the plunge and bought a boat. They are not insuperable problems, but they may be problems.

Experience

Gaining experience in sailing or motorboat handling is now very easy with the recent proliferation of sailing and motor cruising schools. The increase in numbers of schools has largely been due to the widespread acceptance of the Royal Yachting Association's various certificates of competence. These are seen by most people as a sensible way of learning the basic essentials and gaining a good grounding in boat handling and seamanship before plunging into boat ownership.

The Royal Yachting Association is the organising body of boating in Great Britain and does a tremendous amount of work in defending the rights of yachtsmen and in organizing training programmes for beginners. It is well worth joining the RYA, whose Membership Office is at Shaftesbury Road, Gillingham, Dorset SP8 4LJ, and obtaining from their main office at Victoria

Way, Woking, Surrey GU21 1EQ, a list of RYA approved sailing and motorboating schools. These schools run courses leading to the issue of one or other of the RYA's certificates and follow RYA approved training methods and schemes.

The certificates include dinghy and dayboat sailing, coastal cruising, offshore and ocean cruising and motorboat handling. The syllabus for each is comprehensive but not beyond the capabilities of those interested, and having successfully completed one of the courses you can approach ownership of that type of boat with reasonable confidence. You will still need to gain more experience, but at least the groundwork has been done.

It is also possible to gain valuable experience by crewing for other people on their boats. This not only allows you to put in some sea time, but if you get aboard a variety of different boats you will begin to form ideas about what would suit you best.

Cost

At some point you are going to have to consider just how much you can afford to pay for a boat bearing in mind that the outlay of money does not stop when you complete a purchase. It might even be fair to say that that is when the spending begins.

Initially the kind of boat is the over-riding concern and it must be assumed that you have taken a general look at prices and seen that spending so many hundreds or thousands of pounds is not completely impossible, even if a substantial loan (*see* Chapter 8) is required. Thereafter, a lot of shopping around has to be done to discover what is or is not included in the asking price—more of that in Chapter 4—but from the start, beware of VAT. We see the price marked on some item in a shop and it does not occur to us that it includes VAT. With boats, however, the majority of quoted prices (and here we are talking about new boats and equipment) are *exclusive* of VAT which, when added on, bumps the price up horribly. It applies to boats, their equipment, the mooring dues, boatyard services, the lot, so it cannot be ignored.

18

A typical sportsboat suitable for towing water-skiers. This one, powered by an 85hp outboard motor giving very high performance, has an excellent safety feature built into the engine controls—an ignition cut-out. The cord wrapped round the helmsman's wrist is attached to a jack plug which, if jerked out in an emergency, breaks the ignition circuit

When you buy a boat there will always be extra items of gear and equipment that you want to add, so some allowance must be made for these in your calculations. There are also mooring or storage charges, the cost of slipping and launching, paint and varnish, general running costs throughout the season, together with yacht club subscriptions, fuel, travelling and harbour dues. No one in their right mind would actually sit down and work out precisely what a season's boating costs as it would simply be too frightening. On a cost per mile basis there can be few more expensive means of transport, but if you don't do a certain amount of cost analysis you could find yourself in difficulties.

New, secondhand or kit boat?

A rapidly growing number of people are meeting the problem of rising new boat costs by fitting out sets of mouldings, usually the hull and deck bonded together with the structural bulkheads fitted. After buying the mouldings they may choose to work from a set of plans supplied by the builders, design their own accommodation, or install pre-cut units to complete the interior. Building a boat like this does undoubtedly cut the overall cost, but it is not a particularly quick process as few amateurs have either the skill or facilities and tools of the professional boat builder. What you are saving, however, is the cost of professional labour, and if you are cunning and shop around for bargain fittings as well (though watch the quality if they are too cheap) you can save a lot.

There is little doubt that in general a professionally built boat turns out better than an amateur built one as the professional has skills and resources not available to the amateur, and he also takes the time and trouble to 'finish' the boat with trim and cappings to hide such things as the end grain of plywood and unsightly screwheads which many amateurs leave exposed. He knows the tricks of the trade and on a series production boat has a routine for installing things in a certain order to make the job easier. Still, there are a great many sound, seaworthy, home completed boats around, some of them highly 'professional' in finish, so it is perfectly possible for an amateur to do a good job.

A new boat, like a new car, will always have a strong appeal, but when you have selected the kind of boat you want it is time to make a direct comparison between what you get for your money with a new boat and one a few years old. In many cases you would do better to buy a secondhand boat in good condition including some of the extras you want, rather than have a brand-new boat to which you have to add them.

A couple of things to remember about buying secondhand: you will have to pay for a condition survey (*see* Chapter 8) and on an older boat the gear and equipment is likely to need renewal before long. On the other hand, all the bugs which you would have to deal with if you bought a new boat should have been ironed out. Finally, on kit boats, although one or two firms do give help with buying spars, rigging, chandlery and engines, it is often only in the hull and accommodation that you save a lot of money. Thereafter you are likely to have to pay out almost as much as if the boat had been professionally built. You can make some savings by buying carefully and again you avoid labour costs, but the real economy has been made on the hull.

Hull construction materials

The commonest hull construction material today is glassfibre, but wood (in a variety of forms), steel, aluminium and ferro-cement all have their advantages and are widely available. Which material your boat will be built from depends to some extent on the intended use. For instance, there are great advantages in having a steel narrowboat for use on the inland waterways as she will be immensely tough and durable, but for a small coastal cruiser it is a very heavy and rather expensive material.

The advantage of glassfibre for mass production boats is that scores of identical boats can be turned out of one mould in quick succession. A male mould (plug) is first constructed in wood, then a female mould is taken off it in glassfibre and this is used as the mould for all future boats. Glassfibre matt is laid up in the mould and wetted out with resin. When the required thickness of hull has been achieved and it has cured, it is turned out of the mould and the laying up process is begun for the next hull.

Maintenance of glassfibre is less than for other materials as it rarely requires painting for the first five or six years of its life and then not every season as other materials do. A problem known as 'osmosis' or blistering has been discovered, but it is treatable by a paint process and usually relates in seriousness to rot in a wooden boat or the corrosion of steel.

Wood, particularly plywood, is often used by people constructing a boat from scratch, that is from a set of plans but nothing else. Ply is an easy material to work with, but only marine quality should be used in the hull and for that the minimum British standard is BS1088. Other wood construction methods are clinker, where the planks of the hull overlap one another, carvel, where they butt edge to edge, strip planking where narrow planks are edge glued to each other, and cold moulding, where layers of diagonally laid wood veneers are used to build up the required hull thickness. This last method is often used in conjunction with the WEST System of saturating the layers of wood with epoxy resin to exclude water (and more particularly water vapour which can pass through paint), thus preventing rot, and increasing the overall strength dramatically.

The maintenance of a conventional wooden hull is rather more than a glassfibre one needs as it requires painting every season and is susceptible to rot and marine borers (worms). However, the work is not necessarily as much as some people make out, particularly if the hull is well maintained right from the start, and it is undoubtedly a more aesthetically pleasing material than glassfibre. It is interesting that many builders are reverting to all wood interiors after earlier attempts to mask the rather stark, clinical appearance of interior glassfibre mouldings.

Steel is an immensely strong material, but it is rather heavy in the necessary thicknesses for hulls. Its strength is a big advantage for inland waterways boats which tend to get bumped and battered in locks and tunnels, but for sailing and motor cruisers its use is usually confined to craft over 30–35ft where the weight is not so significant. Modern treatments for the bare steel have made the war against rust and corrosion less arduous, but still it must be waged continuously.

Aluminium is still very much a minority choice for hulls but it is light and strong. Like steel it is very easy to suffer from electrolytic corrosion with an aluminium hull if metals are mixed and electrical circuits are set up through the water, so fitting anything—for example seacocks or a speedometer—must be done with care, to insulate each item from the hull. Special primers must also be used under all paintwork. It is a good material for all that and it is likely to become more popular.

When ferrocement began to have a wide use some ten or so years ago there were rather a lot of disastrous amateur attempts at building cheap hulls and as a result the material lost a lot of credence. More recently, however, hulls have been far better built, usually from kits of steel frames, with professionals employed to plaster them to ensure the correct mortar mix and even application. This has produced a lot of excellent hulls, generally heavy displacement ones, but with some very light ones too.

It appears to be a very stable and strong material but it does suffer from the disadvantage of being unsuited to mass production. At least, it is a disadvantage in terms of its widespread use, is no disadvantage in any other way; indeed it has the advantage of being well suited to the construction of one-off boats.

Some dinghies are built in a composite of glassfibre hulls and wooden decks which combination gives the possibility of identical hulls but individual deck layouts. These must generally accord with class rules, but still allow development.

Monohull or multihull?

When considering buying a sailing cruiser you are faced at some stage with the question of whether to buy a boat with one, two or

23

three hulls; that is to say a monohull, a catamaran or a trimaran. The majority of boats are monohulls, but a catamaran offers considerably more internal space than a monohull coupled with the ability to sail faster, upright. This, naturally, has its attractions since life is far more comfortable sailing on an even keel than when thrashing along with the boat well heeled. There are disadvantages though: increased mooring costs and harbour dues, occasional difficulties finding somewhere to slip the boat for winter storage and the unfortunate fact that the boat is just as stable upside down as the right way up. In other words a cat can capsize and remain bottom upwards. With a family cruising cat this is a most unlikely occurence, particularly if reasonable care is taken, but the possibility does deter some people from buying one.

A trimaran also offers great performance in an upright posture, but she will have little more accommodation than an equivalent monohull and may even be more cramped. For the most part the only trimarans on the market are racing tris of very light weight and extremely high speed potential, but there are some cruising ones, notably the Telstar 8m and 11m, and they do offer fast passage making in comfort. Trimarans too will remain upside down if they should turn over, but with a cruising tri it is unlikely to happen. Like cats they also incur higher mooring charges and harbour dues.

There is no hard and fast rule about which kind of boat you should choose, it is entirely a case of looking at what is available, deciding which would suit your needs best and then deciding. Each kind has its good and bad points and these must be weighed up.

Inboard or outboard?

The choice between an inboard and an outboard engine in either a motor or a sailing boat is difficult. An outboard is generally lighter, cheaper than an inboard, is easier to install and can, if necessary, be taken ashore to a mechanic. On a sailing cruiser it is

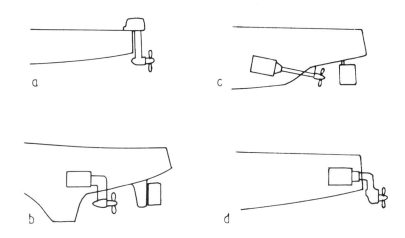

(a) Outboard engine; (b) saildrive; (c) inboard engine; (d) outdrive (inboard/outboard)

a nuisance to have to leave it on the stern when sailing, but it is also awkward to keep taking it on and off. It is for this reason that a number of builders install an outboard motor in a well in the cockpit. With this arrangement the propeller can be lifted clear of the water (so that it does not create drag) and the opening can be sealed with a hatch, but the motor does not have to be removed from its mounting and stored in a locker.

Another recent development is the Saildrive where an inboard engine is connected to what looks something like the lower half of an outboard which passes through the bottom of the boat. In this case you have the power and permanent installation of an inboard with its propeller well immersed (a problem with outboards on the stern in big waves) and easy fitting as the engine and drive unit come in a mounting module that is simply bonded to the hull.

Inboard engines can be either petrol or diesel, the latter often being preferred because of its lower consumption of a generally safer fuel. Petrol engines on the other hand are lighter and cheaper and anyone familiar with the workings of his car ashore can look after the boat's engine, whereas he will probably be unaccustomed to diesel engines.

An inboard is harder to install than an outboard because of the stern gear and cooling system, but it tends to be looked on as a more robust and reliable object—rightly or wrongly—and is always ready for use. The propeller is usually better immersed than that of an outboard, but it does create drag unless a folding or feathering one is fitted. With both of these the blades align themselves with the water flow when not in use.

Some high-speed powerboats and a few canal cruisers are fitted with outdrives which are inboard engines connected through the stern to what look like the lower halves of outboard engines. These drive legs can be lifted up clear of the water when not in use. Such installations allow the engine to be mounted horizontally, rather than on an incline, as the drive is straight out through the stern rather than down through the bottom at an angle.

With a conventional inboard engine a rudder is used to steer the boat, but with an inboard/outboard arrangement the outdrives are turned and the thrust from the propellers steers the boat. This has the disadvantage that the boat cannot be manoeuvred in neutral; there has to be some power applied to give the necessary thrust. With canal cruisers this is a problem as it is normal practice (because it is much easier) to steer gently into a lock in neutral, which can be done with a rudder, but not with outdrives.

The kind of installation finally chosen may be dictated by the space available and the options offered by the builder, but any engine is a costly item and all the possibilities should be studied before a decision is made. Motor cruisers with a single main engine should carry some alternative such as a small get-you-home outboard in case of complete engine failure. Other boats, such as sportsboats, must carry paddles in case of engine breakdown.

The keel

Planing powerboats usually have a vee bottom without any real keel, while displacement motorboats generally have a full-length shallow keel. Sailing craft on the other hand require much more under water to resist leeway when sailing to windward and, in the case of 'keelboats', to carry the essential ballast to counteract the heeling force of the wind on the sails and rigging. Dinghies have either dagger or centreboards, but cruising boats can have full-length keels, fin-and-skeg arrangements, centreplates, twin-bilge keels or triple keels.

The full or long keel with the rudder attached to its after end is now considered old-fashioned, but new designs are still being

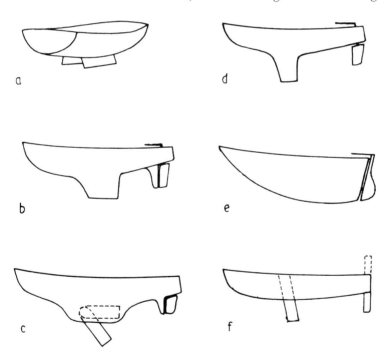

(a) Twin bilge keels; (b) fin keel and skeg hung rudder; (c) centreplate which houses in ballast keel; (d) fin keel and spade rudder; (e) full keel and transom hung rudder; (f) lifting keel and rudder

produced with this keel configuration as it has certain attractive qualities. In the first place it is the strongest keel and rudder structure; secondly it is usually coupled with heavier displacement which can give an easier motion in a seaway; thirdly there is less chance of ropes lodging anywhere or fouling the propeller which is well guarded in an aperture in the keel just ahead of the rudder. A long keel can also give the boat greater directional stability than a fin and separate rudder, but this is not necessarily so and similarly, it is usually, but not always, easier to dry out safely alongside a wall with a long-keeled boat. When manoeuvring, the boat with a long keel turns more slowly than her fin-keeled sister and when going astern under power it may not be possible to steer her other than in a straight line.

Most modern designs have a fin keel with a separate rudder, either a spade rudder or a skeg rudder. The former simply hangs beneath the boat on its own stock (the shaft connecting it to the tiller) and the latter is carried on the after end of a supporting bracket (skeg) fixed to the hull.

A fin keel and separate rudder create much less wetted surface area (and hence drag) than a full keel and rudder, but ultimately they are likely to be structurally weaker. The boat will be more sensitive to movement of the rudder and so will require more concentration by the helmsman. She will be of light displacement which will make her fast, but rather lively in a seaway. One great advantage for the family is that a modern fin-and-skeg design will have greater internal space than a more traditional boat of the same overall length. This has nothing to do with her type of keel, it is just that modern glassfibre designs are beamier with greater freeboard and no internal space is taken up with large ribs or deck beams. Drying out alongside must be undertaken with caution as the foot of the keel is short and the boat may tip by the head or stern, particularly if anyone moves about on deck.

The centreplate or lifting keel faded from popularity but is currently undergoing a revival. The great advantage is that the boat can be moored in shallow water yet the depth of keel can be

The Hunter Medina is a lifting-keel trailer sailer designed as a complete unit with a fitted launching trolley which rides piggy-back on her road trailer, thus avoiding the problems of immersing the road trailer when launching or recovering the boat. Twenty-feet overall, she has simple accommodation for four

increased greatly for sailing to windward in open water. Boats with a lifting keel which retracts completely can dry out virtually upright, but in this case the box housing the keel will intrude into the accommodation. On the other hand, a centreplate which houses in a stub keel leaves the cabin unobstructed but causes the boat to take the ground at some angle of heel—less than with a fixed keel, but nevertheless uncomfortable.

Undoubtedly the boat to have for drying moorings is one with bilge keels, either twin-ballasted ones or a central-ballast stub keel and bilge plates on either side. With one of these arrangements the boat can sit upright—at least on a level bottom—and is completely habitable. She may not be quite as close winded as a boat of the same class fitted with a fin keel, but the difference is usually negligible and overall performance is not impaired.

In general terms then, choice of keel is largely dictated by the kind of mooring the boat will be kept on and the waters in which she will sail. If she is to sail in shoal waters then either bilge keels or a lifting keel would be sensible, while in areas of deep water a fin or long keel might be better.

The rig

Few production boats today are rigged as anything other than bermudan sloops. There are some bermudan ketches or yawls on the market, one or two bermudan cutters and a handful of gaff cutters or ketches, but they are all very much minority exceptions to the rule. A resurgence of interest in traditional style craft, based loosely on working boat lines, has brought a revival of gaff rig, but for many people its advantages are outweighed by its complexity. It is the simplicity of bermudan rig that is perhaps its greatest virtue, requiring as it does only a single halyard and sheet for each sail, unlike the throat halyard, peak halyard, runners and so on associated with gaff rig.

Bermudan sloop rig is most efficient when sailing to windward. Off the wind it loses out to gaff rig unless supplemented by a spinnaker, which is not an easily handled sail in strong winds.

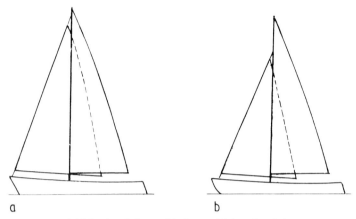

(a) Masthead sloop; (b) sloop with fractional rig

However, as any rig has both good and bad points, it is perhaps sufficient to say that you are most likely to end up with a bermudan rigged boat and the main thing is to examine the arrangement of the various sheets and lines to decide whether or not the sails will be easy to set, hand, reef and trim. This can best be done by going out for a trial sail as will be discussed in Chapter 7.

2 WHERE TO LOOK

Once the decision to buy a boat has been made, whether she is to be a brand-new boat or a 'secondhand' one—which may mean anything from second to sixteenth hand—the problem arises of where to find the kind of boat you have decided on. Initially the best thing to do is examine the various yachting magazines dealing with your chosen aspect of the sport, since it is in these magazines that boat builders, yacht brokers and private owners do most of their advertising. If you don't already read the relevant magazines on a regular basis, now is the time to start.

Such advertising is split into two kinds—display and classified advertisements. Display ads are the province of boat builders and equipment manufacturers and are the ones that use photographs, often in full colour, of their boats or gear and equipment. In other words they deal with new boats. The classified ads are the small ones usually at the back of the magazine where private owners run a few lines describing their boat and stating the asking price.

Whether you are after a new, secondhand or kit boat, it is worth studying both lots of advertisements because the display ones will (or should) give you a certain amount of basic information about the particular boat being advertised, while the classified ads may give you an idea of how that class holds their price and how readily available they are secondhand. In the case of a completely new design you won't be able to make such a comparison and must rely on your own judgement.

When a particular class of boat catches your eye as a possible solution to your requirements, even if you intend eventually to buy a secondhand example of the design, it is worth contacting the builders and asking for full details to be sent to you. Don't waste their time and money by asking for brochures on boats that are not serious possibilities, but equally, don't hesitate to make enquiries about ones that are. They realize that only a proportion of enquiries result in sales and will treat your request for information as seriously as any other; after all if you buy one of their boats secondhand now and like her, you may come back for a new one later, perhaps even a bigger one, and your satisfaction may rub off on other potential customers. Many advertisements have a cutout coupon on which you write your name and address and send it off for details to be sent to you. Doing this, rather than writing a letter, is both easier for you and more helpful to the builder as he can then keep a check on how many enquiries have resulted from that advertisement, hence how well he is spending his money. The magazine will like it too as the advertiser knows which one the coupon comes from. Really this has nothing to do with choosing and buying a boat, but it does promote the business in general and that in the end is good for you.

After you have received details of the boat and have had time to study them, if you have a couple of queries about some details, again don't hesitate—provided that you are serious—to ring the builders and ask your questions. The bigger yards have permanent sales staff available to answer just such calls. They will inevitably try to persuade you that their boat is the one for you, but accepting that (they do have a job to do) they can be very helpful. They know pretty well all of the competing boats on the market and should be able to tell you how and why they chose a particular method to overcome any problems that seem to you to have been approached by quite different paths on other boats. They can discuss options on gear and equipment such as engines and sails. A good firm, even if you come clean and admit that you are really looking for a secondhand boat, should still give you their time and help since public goodwill is all important in this industry and there's always the chance that one day you may

The Sonata 7 is a one-design cruiser racer offering class or handicap racing and comfortable cruising for four people. Like the Medina (p 29), she is designed by David Thomas and so many Sonatas now enter for Cowes Week that the class has been given its own races

want a new boat and then you will remember who was helpful and who was not. Don't take advantage of them, but make the most of it; advice is all that you will get free.

Understanding advertisements

Though fewer abbreviations are used in classified ads today it is still necessary to learn some of the basic ones to understand just what is being said. Many of the manufacturers' or trade names will become familiar from looking through the display ads, so that when you see a boat listed as having 'six sails (Hood, North and Banks)', you will recognise these as being the names of the sailmakers. Similarly you will soon come to realise that a boat with 'full B&G' is equipped with a range (though not always as complete as 'full' would have you think) of Brookes & Gatehouse electronic instruments, such as echosounder, log, wind speed and direction, radio direction finder, and so on, or that a dinghy with 'Needlespar' has a mast and boom made by that firm.

In general it is fair to make certain assumptions if nothing is stated to the contrary: most modern sailing boats are bermudan sloops with Terylene sails set on aluminium anodized alloy spars. Also the majority of smaller boats are tiller steered.

If, at the beginning of a classified ad it says, E7963, N1480, OK 1671, Laser 59895 or some such abbreviation and number, it is referring to the class of dinghy and her sail number. These examples are, in order, an Enterprise, a National 12, an OK dinghy and a Laser, but there are inumerable dinghy classes so a full list is impossible. Most, fortunately, have names such as Fireball or Cherub so identification in an ad is easier.

In the Appendix there is a list of common terms and abbreviations used in classified boat ads.

Going to a broker

Yacht brokers do not normally deal with dinghies, but for larger sailing and motor boats they can be a most effective way of seeking out and buying a boat of the type you are after. A few of the larger brokers deal with boats not only all over the country but all over the world; however, the majority of brokers are smaller concerns concentrating their efforts on a particular locality or occasionally a certain type of craft. This cuts both ways: it does mean that you have to chase brokers all over the place if you want to spread the net wide, but on the other hand it does also mean that you can go to a local man and know that he will produce boats that do not entail too much expensive travelling to view and ultimately can be brought to your home port without great difficulty.

Brokers are in the business of selling boats and they will therefore go to some trouble to help you if they think you are likely to buy through them. They make their money by charging the vendor (that is the owner who is selling the boat) a percentage of the selling price; they do not charge you, the purchaser. We will say more about their job in Chapter 8, but for the moment, so far as finding a boat is concerned, it is helpful to go and talk to a broker and discuss your hopes and aspirations with him. Once you have given him a clear idea of the kind of boat you are looking for and the amount of money you are prepared (able) to spend, he should be able to provide you with details of a few craft that are at least close to your ideal. Assuming that none of these is exactly what you want he will then put you on his mailing list and will send you details of possible boats as and when they come onto his books. Just like an estate agent really and just like an estate agent he will send you details of boats whose asking price is above your limit—no broker (or estate agent) ever seems to believe what you tell him about money!

One very useful facet of going to a broker if you are not completely sure of your requirements is that you can use him as something of a sounding board to bounce your ideas off. He is well acquainted with the problems of choosing a suitable boat and should be able to give you a lot of constructive help and advice.

Boatyards

A lot of larger boatyards run a brokerage section and may have some of the boats on their books actually lying in their yard for immediate inspection or on one of their moorings. This makes it very simple to take a quick look at what's available and to discuss the boats with the broker. On the other hand, smaller yards may have a few boats for sale without actually running a full brokerage service. Gone are the days when yard managers showed a distinct lack of enthusiasm for showing anyone over a boat that was for sale but rather went and hid behind a pile of seasoning timber till you went away. It's a hard commercial world now and boatyards, like every other business, have to do their best to assist the serious customer. Even the smallest yard will have a notice board somewhere with fading, mis-spelt cards pinned up giving details of a handful of assorted craft for sale and it's always worthwhile finding the guv'nor and talking with him. He may have a file of boats for sale and may know of someone or other who might be thinking of selling at the end of the season. With these yards there are always a lot of ifs, buts, maybes and mights, but they often come up with the right boat in the end.

If you go to a boatyard in the area you are hoping to keep the boat eventually it is a good time to broach the subject of moorings. Even if they say you haven't a hope of getting one, at least you know. Usually, however, they are rather more positive; even if they have to say they can't help you themselves they can usually point you in the right direction for finding one.

Noticeboards

Apart from the noticeboards outside boatyard offices, clubhouses usually have a member's noticeboard where people pin up cards advertising all sorts of things from shackles to boats and back again. If you are a member of the club it is easy enough to keep an eye on the board and watch to see if a suitable boat comes up, but for non-members it is a case of asking the steward or someone on duty in the bar for permission to take a look. Few clubs will object, and if you are a member of another club you can legitimately ask to sign the visitors' book, have a drink in the bar and perhaps talk to one or two members, enquiring if they know of any boats for sale that would meet your requirements.

Newsagents and confectioners often have noticeboards outside and these too can provide a useful source of boats, mostly dinghies, angling boats and smaller launches and sportsboats. Things like outboard motors too are often advertised and if you are in the market for one they may be cheaper here than elsewhere.

Chandlers too may provide noticeboards outside and again you will find everything from lifejackets and oilskins to quite large boats. Don't forget such noticeboards even after you have bought your boat if you require extra gear and equipment. If you are careful you can pick up some good stuff at reasonable prices, usually far below the cost of a new item.

Non-boating press

Exchange & Mart is a favourite source of boats and boating equipment of all types. At one time there were some real bargains to be had from its columns, but now it seems that owners are more aware of the true value of their boats and gear. Still, you will find the more unusual items that are not advertised elsewhere. If you need a tender this is always a good place to look, but beware when buying items of gear and equipment that they are genuinely the vendor's property. It's a nasty fact that the steady trade in stolen boat gear occasionally finds an outlet through advertisements in magazines and newspapers. This is no reflection on the publication as there is no possible way they can check the veracity of all advertisements, particularly classified ones, but it is something to be aware of for you stand to lose all title to the purchase if it turns out to have been stolen.

Local newspapers too have sections of classified ads in which you may find a few boats for sale, particularly in papers covering a boating area. Just occasionally the large and expensive types of motor yacht are to be found in the columns of the national newspapers, but these are not common.

Auctions

While it is possible to pick up a boat at a bargain price from a boat auction it is a risky business as you are buying her 'as seen'. That is to say with all her faults. You do not have the chance to call in a surveyor to examine her condition, all you can do is poke about as best you are able and bid accordingly. I would not recommend such a process to anyone who is a newcomer to boating and would advise caution for anyone who is not an experienced surveyor. It was not at an auction, but I very nearly bought a bad boat once and it was only the surveyor that saved me a very costly

This Impala is one of a new breed of yachts known as Offshore One Designs, of which there are three official types: the Impala 28, Offshore One Design 34 and the 101. The idea was to produce keen class racing where changes in the offshore rating rule would not make boats obsolete. The aim seems to have been achieved and fleets are growing quickly mistake. I had examined the boat thoroughly and could find little wrong, but the surveyor discovered that the core of the plywood with which the hull was constructed was badly rotted, leaving little more than an outer and inner veneer. A salutory experience if ever there was one.

Word of mouth

Once you start looking for a boat, particularly if you belong to a yacht club and mention the fact in the bar a couple of times, you may find that people will tell you of boats for sale, or indeed approach you as a possible buyer of their own boats. As with all boat buying you must be wary, particularly if the owner is a friend. Still, it's always worth keeping your ears open as a good boat can be sold very quickly and if you wait until she is advertised you may find someone else has slipped in and bought her. This probably happens more often with successful racing dinghies, but it's annoying.

Boat shows

So far as new boats are concerned, boat shows are valuable to the potential buyer as he can see a variety of possible boats virtually next door to each other and make immediate comparisons. You can also go round and price all the extra equipment you will need if you buy a new boat since there are always a large number of gear and equipment manufacturers exhibiting as well as boat builders.

I can never quite make up my mind whether I would rather see a boat at a show in the water or out of it. In the water you can gain some idea of how she looks afloat in terms of appearance and trim, and also feel how she lies in harbour, but out of the water you can have a good look at her underwater hull form, keel and rudder. I suppose it's six of one and half a dozen of the other.

A few builders will take boats in part-exchange for new ones particularly where someone is moving up to a larger boat in their range. Thus, if you are interested in a particular class of boat but have decided on a secondhand one, it may be worth asking the builder if he has or knows of any secondhand ones for sale. If he has taken a boat in part-exchange and can sell her to you he will be happy and you could have solved your problem.

Before going to a boat show try to decide what boats you want to have a look over and on arrival go round making appointments to view. It is unfortunate that with the immense number of visitors to boat shows it has been necessary for many companies to introduce 'viewing by appointment only' as people would otherwise be queuing for hours to get aboard. It's extremely frustrating to have to book, but at least it does guarantee you a good look at the boat.

Just as you should not write to or phone builders and pester them, don't go round boat shows collecting brochures for the sake of doing so, but if you are genuinely interested in a boat after seeing her 'in the flesh' as it were, be sure to get all the information available. Also, if you can, make a note of the name of the salesman you talked to so that if you want to find out anything else you will know who to telephone or write to after the show is over.

Computer listings

There are one or two firms now operating computer data banks providing basic information on boats for sale together with the names and addresses of their owners. These firms do not act in the same way as brokers; they are more akin to classified advertisements. An owner pays a single flat fee for his boat to be put on the computer list and that's it. The firm does not take a percentage of the selling price or anything else. A prospective purchaser contacts the computer firm, specifies his requirements and is sent a list of possible boats together with the owners' names and addresses. Thereafter it becomes a private transaction in the same way as if the purchaser had seen a classified ad or heard about the boat by word of mouth. The computer firm takes no further part in the deal and probably never even sees the boat.

3 DOWN TO DETAILS

Once you have sorted out the general problem of what kind of boat you want to buy—motor cruiser, racing dinghy, canal boat or whatever—it is time to get down to more detailed consideration of the alternative hulls, layouts, equipment and fittings available.

The first question to consider, and it's not an easy one to answer, is that of what size of boat to buy. If you live in a house with a garden or even in a largish flat, any boat is likely to seem relatively small and cramped, so the natural tendency is to look for as large a boat as you can get for your money. This, however, may not be the right thing to do as she will be expensive to run and maintain, harder work to handle than a smaller boat and if she is too big, you may even be dependent on other people forming a crew to allow you to take her out. You may *want* to have other people on board, but being dependent on them puts severe strictures on your enjoyment. Equally there is no point in having a boat so small you continually fall over yourself when you can afford a boat rather larger. So what's the best compromise?

To answer that question you have to answer several others. How many people do you expect to be aboard regularly? How long do you plan to stay aboard on the average trip and how long do you think holiday trips will be? What proportion of the crew can be classed as fit to handle the boat and/or stand a watch in their own right? Is the crew to be family only or will you have guests aboard on a fairly regular basis? The physical strength of the crew must also be considered on a sailing boat as the work of

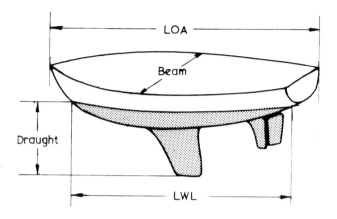

Principal dimensions

sail handling, anchoring and so forth can be arduous despite winches and other aids.

If the plan is for a couple plus say two or three children to cruise at weekends with a summer holiday of a fortnight afloat, the boat need be no more than 30ft and can be less, but if you intend taking extra crew with you all the time, then that boat must grow to about 40ft. It is one thing sharing a small space with minimal privacy when the rest of the crew are members of your family, but it can be quite another when they are outsiders, possibly even relative strangers. This matter of privacy, or rather lack of privacy, is something that has to be approached with caution even in family circumstances and every effort must be made to afford the individual whatever privacy is possible, even if it only amounts to turning a blind eye or deaf ear. It's all part of the important process of learning to 'live small' when you take to cruising.

When you get down to comparing individual designs, the dimensions of a boat can help to give you an idea of her shape and space. The principle dimensions are length overall (LOA), load waterline length (LWL), beam and draught. For all practical purposes the overall length can be taken as the boat's length from stem to stern, excluding any bowsprit or other projection. The

43

difference in length between a boat's LOA and her LWL indicates the length of overhang she has at bow and stern. So far as accommodation is concerned this overhanging length is largely wasted, consequently it is the LWL that gives a better idea of her living space than the LOA. Beam too comes into it as the greater the vessel's beam the greater her internal volume, but there is more to it than that. A look at a few boat plans will show that a boat with massive maximum beam but pinched in ends may have less real accommodation than a narrower boat with her beam continued well fore and aft.

There is also today an enormous difference between a sailing cruiser's total draught (ie from waterline to foot of keel) and the depth of her hull below the waterline. Most sailing boats are now given very shallow, flat-bottomed hulls which mean internal height must be increased by raising the topsides and deck structure, whereas in older boats the sole could be dropped down into the bilges, increasing internal height without increasing freeboard. Thus, when comparing designs offering very good internal height, study the way this has been achieved and see if it is acceptable to you, remembering that freeboard and tophamper can make low-speed handling more awkward and boarding from a dinghy difficult.

Your proposed boating area or activity may also put certain restrictions on the chosen boat's dimensions: a drying or shallow water mooring; beam limited by lock widths on the inland waterways to 7ft; clearance under a bridge without having to lower the mast. Size is more than just a matter of finding out how big a boat £X,000 will buy.

Hull form

While the LOA, beam and draught measurements of a vessel go some way towards describing her, two boats of similar dimensions can be amazingly different when seen as three-dimensional shapes. One may have her maximum beam continued well fore and aft while the other concentrates it at one point with the ends

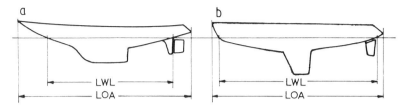

(a) Long overhangs: big difference between LOA and LWL; (b) short overhangs: little difference between LOA and LWL

pinched right in. One boat may have a wide transom stern while the other has a canoe stern or long reversed counter. One hull may be of deep V form while the other is a cathedral type. Each of these differences is enough to make considerable changes in the boat's usefulness, performance, accommodation and handling.

So far as fast planing and semi-displacement motor boats are concerned, the deep V hull form has become prevalent as it offers a comparatively soft ride while maintaining good planing surfaces aft. So what is deep V? Literally the hull under water is like a capital V when viewed from the bow. We say the hull has high deadrise, that is the angle between the bottom and the ground when standing ashore and again viewed from ahead. The sharpness of the vee allows the hull to cut down into a sea thus making a soft landing rather than slamming onto a flat surface. It is an interesting fact that as quickly as deep V became popular for

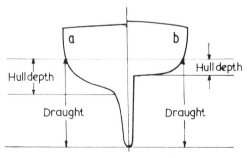

(a) Old boat has hull depth equalling about 40–50% of total draught; (b) modern light displacement boat has hull depth amounting to only about 20% of the total draught

45

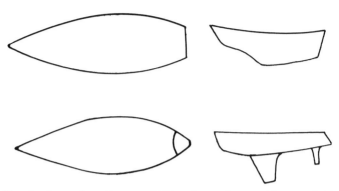

Two boats may have the same LOA and same beam yet be completely different shapes

powerboats, so it faded from fashion for sailing boats as they sought after reduced wetted surface area. It is only a highly powered craft that can make use of the deep V sections for the relatively snail-like sailing boat simply slices through waves soaking her crew. With low weight and low underwater wetted surface area the flat-bottomed sailing boat moves much faster but with a livelier motion.

The modern trend in sailing boats towards canoe-like underwater sections has produced faster boats than their long-keeled heavy displacement older sisters, but they are far more skittish and require greater effort to get the most out of them. This is not necessarily a bad thing; it is simply another factor to consider when choosing a boat. If you are moving out of dinghies into a family boat you may well want the better performance of one of

$\emptyset$ = angle of 'deadrise' of a deep vee hull

46

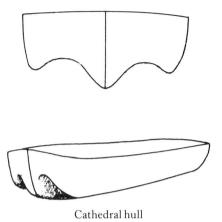

Cathedral hull

these craft, but on the other hand, if you are buying a boat when your children have grown up and left home you may require something a trifle more comfortable and will be able to accept a slightly inferior performance.

When trying to compare possible boats you have to look at the hull form of each and try to determine why she has been designed in that way and what advantages it offers you. If you can't come up with a satisfactory answer you will have to consult the builders, but there must be an answer.

Keels

A large number of sailing cruisers and cruiser/racers are offered with an option on the kind of keel configuration used. This is usually a choice of either fin or bilge keels or a centreplate. The pros and cons of these types have been discussed in Chapter 1, but if you decide you want to have some keel arrangement other than the standard one you must be very careful to check that the necessary structural changes will be made. After all, without going into detail, it should be clear that if a boat is designed to have a fin keel and you opt for twin keels, the stresses on the hull are going to be different and they will be transmitted to different parts of the hull; consequently the strengthening of the hull in those areas must be altered.

47

A Shearwater 22-footer under storm jib and well-reefed main with her cockpit 'dodgers' displaying her name clearly and protecting the helmsman from some of the spray that will be flying shortly. At the moment she is in sheltered water, but she is making out into some rough open water and her skipper has had the good sense and foresight to snug her down while the going is relatively easy

Although this revamping of the structural arrangements can be done perfectly successfully, I think if it ever came down to a straight choice between two boats, of which one was designed for the keel form I wanted and the other was not but offered that arrangement as an alternative, I would choose the one designed for the job. However, the odds are that there would be other considerations as well—there usually are.

So far as lifting keels are concerned, there are many different types and choice between them is not easy. In the first place there are keels that retract completely into the boat leaving a flush bottom to the hull while others house in an exterior ballast keel so as not to intrude into the accommodation, and others again lift partly into a ballast stub and partly into an internal case. Which to choose?

The boats with some external keel may be sailed with the keel lifted, albeit with impaired performance, while those with keels that raise right into the boat can only be sailed with the keel lowered. They can, however, float in considerably shallower water and when they finally dry out they will do so in a more upright attitude. This has advantages if the boat is kept on a drying mooring and if launching and recovering from a trailer is to be done at all frequently since the trailer will not have to be put so far into the water and positioning the boat on it in shallow water will be easier.

You must also decide how much the intrusion of the keel box into the cabin matters. If the boat was designed initially as a centreboarder it may be used as a part of the layout, but if it is an alternative, then it may be intrusive and a real nuisance. It need not intrude at all, in either instance, and so much the better if that is the situation, but look and consider it. Also look at and consider the hoist system. Some are more robust than others; some are more complicated than others; some can be inspected and have the hoist cables replaced with the boat afloat; some require the boat to be dried out. Stones jamming between the plate and its case often cause problems. Has provision been made for clearing them?

49

A distinction should be made here between centreplates and lifting keels. Centreplates are simple sheets of cast iron or steel and constitute only a small proportion of the boat's total ballast, while a lifting keel is much heavier and constitutes a high proportion of the total ballast if not all of it. The boat with a centreplate normally has an external stub-ballast keel which may house the plate entirely, while the lifting-keel boat generally has internal ballast (unless the keel forms the total ballast). Centreplate boats can therefore often sail to windward (in a limited fashion) with the plate housed, but lifting-keel boats cannot. With a centreplate raised there is little change in the boat's stability, whereas with a lifting keel raised there may be a great change as the centre of gravity will be considerably higher. This need not be dangerous, but on a light boat with the keel providing all of the ballast it can make movement on board rather un-nerving.

The lifting system for either plate or keel also requires careful attention. It must be easy to operate and should be no more complicated than is absolutely necessary. It should be easily accessible too, both for operation and maintenance or repair.

Displacement

The term displacement is used in two ways: in one context it describes a type of hull and in the other it is a straightforward measurement of the boat's weight. Motor boats are classed as having either displacement, semi-displacement or planing hulls, while sailing boats, other than planing dinghies, all have displacement hulls. Some racing boats manage to come close to

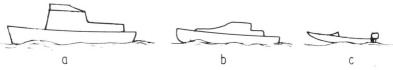

a   b   c

(a) Displacement motor cruiser, cruising speed probably less than 10 knots; (b) semi-displacement motor cruiser with top speed of about 15–20 knots; (c) planing sports boat of kind often used for water skiing, offers speeds as high as 30 knots

planing and sail in a semi-displacement attitude, but they are really of displacement form.

A displacement hull, however hard it is pushed, remains completely in the water and has an upper speed limit related to the waterline length. A semi-displacement hull can be driven so that the stern sinks and the bow begins to rise out of the water, thus achieving a speed higher than the theoretical limit for an equivalent displacement hull. Finally, a planing hull goes all the way and rises up to travel on her own bow wave, thus reaching speeds far in excess of her displacement sisters. The ability to achieve this state is directly related to hull form and weight (displacement), a planing hull being far lighter than a displacement one.

If you choose to buy an open sportsboat for water-skiing or a racing dinghy, you will certainly buy a planing boat, but if you are more interested in motor cruising you will have to decide which hull type to go for. Displacement boats are slower than semi-displacement ones which are in turn slower than planing ones. Displacement hulls usually have more economical engines fitted than the others. As to sea-keeping qualities, there need not be a lot of difference if the boats are well designed—just like light and heavy displacement sailing cruisers—but the lighter boats may have a more violent motion. They do, however, have the big advantage that their high speed and additional engine power usually allows them to seek shelter before bad weather closes in.

Turning to displacement where it means the weight of a boat, the majority of family sailing cruisers built today can be described as being of medium displacement, leaving the really light boats for top-class racing and the heavy displacement boats mainly for ocean cruising. Light boats are also sailed long distances, but heavy displacement ones are seldom raced. The family cruiser, if well prepared, will be capable of remaining at sea in bad weather, but certainly her crew will be far happier if they have managed either to make port or stay in port to avoid the rough stuff.

What it boils down to for the potential motor boat buyer is

A Laser singlehanded dinghy with her crew sitting well out to keep her sailing upright and fast. Lasers are tremendously popular boats with over 80,000 afloat. They are rigidly one design with every item of gear the same on each boat, which makes winning races purely a matter of the crew's ability

probable usage of the boat. If most of your time will be spent on the inland waterways there is no point in buying a planing power cruiser as she will be unhappy at permanently slow speeds. On the other hand, if you are planning to make weekend coastal passages, there is a lot to be said in favour of a high speed planing cruiser which can go further in a given time or take a shorter time to cover a set distance, thus allowing more time in harbour where, perhaps, children will have the chance to go ashore or play on a beach.

Tonnage

It used to be common practice to describe a boat by her Thames Measurement tonnage which was an old rating system for racing, long defunct, relying heavily for its calculation on the boat's beam. This gave a satisfactory description of a boat for those familiar with wooden boats of planked construction and long keels, but it is quite unsuited to modern boats and we tend to talk now in terms of actual weight (displacement). This can be measured in tons, tonnes, pounds or kilos according to preference.

Other tonnages, such as registered, gross and net register tonnage, are mainly applied to ships but also have to be worked out when a yacht is to be registered. These tonnages have nothing to do with weight but refer in effect to cargo carrying space. A registered ton is 100 cubic feet of internal space; the gross tonnage is the registered tonnage measured below decks plus the capacity of deckhouses and other superstructures; net register tonnage is the gross tonnage less allowances for non-earning space such as engines, tanks, stores and crew's accommodation.

Finally, the other 'tons' referred to are Two Ton, One Ton, ¾ Ton, ½ Ton, ¼ Ton, Mini Ton and Micro Ton, all of which are (like the old Thames Measurement) part of a handicapping system for offshore racing. A highly complex formula is used to derive a rating of so many feet and according to that figure the boat fits into a particular 'Ton' category and is eligible for racing in boat-for-boat competition with others of her size.

Sail plans

Comparison of sail plans is by no means an easy aspect of looking objectively at possible boats. A designer can do various calculations to determine the sail area required to drive the hull efficiently, but they are far too complex for most laymen. With experience you can look at a sail plan and say whether or not the boat will be under-canvassed and whether or not she is likely to be well balanced, but these are rather vague conclusions. Of more practical value is a comparison of how the sail area is split between mainsail and headsail (plus mizzen if so rigged) to decide whether they are easily managed sails.

Again it is impossible to put an exact figure on what sail area can be handled by one person, but if the boat is drawn with a tiny mainsail and very large masthead genoas, then you can be sure that foredeck work is going to be frequent and possibly arduous. Certainly you will require good winches to sheet the larger genoas in hard. If, on the other hand, the headsails are of moderate size and the mainsail compares favourably, then there is little to worry about.

Few, if any, production boats designed for family use are over-canvassed, but they all need to be equipped with good reefing systems since this task is more than likely to be left rather late and will probably be carried out singlehanded by the skipper as he won't want any of his crew risking their safety by being on a lurching deck. Such a mainsail reefing system does not depend on its *type* for its 'goodness', rather on its arrangement.

The two types in general use are roller reefing and slab or 'jiffy' reefing. The former involves rolling the sail round the boom by various means and the latter lowering a section of the sail onto the boom and tying it down. With roller reefing any amount of sail can be removed; with slab reefing only set chunks can be taken out. A poorly arranged roller reefing system allows the end of the boom to droop until it may actually foul the cabin top, but if properly designed and arranged this can be avoided.

For roller reefing the mainsail there are two systems, one

54

involving a worm gear built into the end of the boom at the goose-neck which revolves the boom when operated by a crank handle, and the other in which a 'through-mast' drive is used to revolve the boom. The worm-drive system is slower because the worm acts as a reduction gear whereas the through-mast system is 'direct drive'—one revolution of the handle produces one revolution of the boom. With either system the sail has to be taken away from its attachment to the mast, either having the slides taken out of the track or the luff rope (or tape) taken out of the groove. Thus, when the reef is shaken out, the slides or tape must be fed back in as the sail is re-hoisted.

It is impossible to say which is the better system because if they are well arranged then they both do their job adequately. The problem of boom droop with some roller reefing can be overcome by proper boom shaping and the way the sail is cut. The real point is that whichever system is used it must be well planned, preferably for operation by one person. That means having the halyard and reefing lines or reefing handle operable from the same position, since with roller reefing it helps to maintain some tension on the halyard as the boom is revolved and with slab reefing the halyard needs to be retensioned (set up) as soon as the luff is hooked down otherwise the cringle will fall off the hook. We will say something about trying out the reefing system in Chapter 7.

Steering gear

Although tiller steering is still the commonest form of steering gear for sailing boats, it is by no means unusual to find a boat of 30ft or less fitted with wheel steering. A lot of builders offer a choice of tiller or wheel and which you choose is a matter of personal preference.

A lot of people find wheel steering less sensitive than a tiller and have difficulty in sailing the boat as efficiently or on such an accurate course. However, on larger boats it is lighter work steering with a wheel. For motor boats it is unusual to find tiller steer-

The Mirror dinghy, a build-her-yourself design sponsored by the *Daily Mirror* newspaper, has probably started more people sailing, both adults and children, than even the International Cadet (pp 12, 14, 15). At 10ft 10in she is simple to build and can be sailed under mainsail alone, without the jib, by children. The boat shown here needs her halyards set up harder to remove the creases from both sails

ing on anything other than an open launch or narrowboat-style canal cruiser. It is generally found to be easier controlling a canal boat with a tiller and rudder rather than with a wheel, particularly in the close quarters manoeuvring required on entering and leaving locks.

Whatever steering gear is used it must be accessible for maintenance and repair. The wire cables employed in some wheel steering systems must run over large diameter sheaves and must have fair leads into and out of them. The wires must never be kinked or allowed to chafe either on each other or on some part of the boat.

One final word of warning about wheels: if they are of plain stainless steel they will be dreadfully cold on the hands in only slightly cold weather.

Engine and controls

Although there has been a tremendous swing towards the use of diesel engines, the choice between petrol or diesel is still a very difficult one. The price of both fuels has increased substantially in the last few years and the savings made by the lower consumption of diesel are no longer as great as they used to be. This is particularly applicable if you are thinking of recovering the difference in initial engine cost by this saving. The price difference between diesel and petrol engines is substantial and when the amount of annual usage is taken into consideration, it would take many, many seasons to recover the difference in outlay.

Diesel is undoubtedly a safer fuel to carry on a boat, but with a certain amount of care there is no reason why petrol should be inordinately dangerous. Many people maintain their own car engines and they will be able to cope with petrol boat engine problems far more easily than they would diesel ones. On the other hand, petrol engines rely heavily on electrics while diesels, if they can be hand-started, do not require any electrics and in a marine environment, which is hostile to electrics, that is a great advantage.

It is a strange fact that people who would insist on a diesel inboard engine are perfectly happy to carry the supposedly dangerous petrol for a dinghy outboard engine in a decidedly dangerous old one gallon oil can.

Comparison of reliability of the two types of engine is not easy as the usual cause of trouble with petrol engines, as already mentioned, is an electrical fault or incorrect petrol/oil mixture in a two stroke engine, whereas the problems encountered with diesels are mainly air in the fuel lines or dirt in them. With good installation such problems are avoidable—or at least their occurence can be greatly reduced—but it is up to you which you feel better able to combat.

The option may also exist of having an outboard engine, some advantages of which were discussed in Chapter 1, and when comparing possible boats it is one of the items to check and note.

Engine controls also need consideration, not only their operation but their siting. The majority of boats use either single lever controls to operate both gears and throttle or twin levers (one gear and one throttle) but in the same unit remote from the engine. Only in work boats is it common to find a genuine gear lever acting directly on the gearbox.

Whichever gear and throttle system is used, and the single lever does seem to be simpler, the controls must be readily accessible to the helmsman without being sited so close to the compass that they interfere with its accuracy. In an open cockpit they can be fitted in a moulded recess in the side of the foot well, for example. This keeps them away from the compass and reduces the chances of their being kicked, stepped on or caught up in trouser ends. Again you must check accessibility for maintenance and repair.

Cockpits

It is rare to find a cockpit that is not self-draining, but some are more self-draining than others. A lot of cockpit drains are so small that they act as little more than rain drains. If they are to be any good when most needed, in the hopefully rare event of filling by a wave, they must be of large diameter without grids over their openings. These grids, such as are used in household sink drains, are good for stopping debris blocking up the pipes, but they seriously reduce the open area of the drain. It is far better to have large pipes and openings which can be unblocked by a plunger or rod of some sort.

Whatever drains are provided, they must have seacocks fitted where they pass through the hull. If this is not done and something happens to the pipe it is difficult to close the outlet which will suddenly become a substantial inlet for seawater.

Some centreboard boats have a cunning system of leading cockpit and sink drains into the centreboard case to avoid drilling more holes in the hull than necessary. This makes a lot of sense and appears to work well.

If part of the engine access is by way of lifting part of the cockpit sole, check that the hatch is capable of being made watertight or the advantages of the self-draining cockpit will be lost. The engine may also be drowned.

Racing dinghies are usually fitted with self-bailers in the bottom of the boat or with transom flaps to clear water. Both of these systems are more efficient than the self-draining of larger boats' cockpits and rightly so as they are intended to clear not only spray but all the water gathered during a capsize and subsequent righting.

Berths

Most boats have rather fewer berths suitable for use at sea than the total number available when in port. This is partly because the motion of the boat is at its greatest in the forward part of the vessel and hence the forecabin berths frequently become untenable simply because the occupants can't stand the motion and are sick. The convertible dinette/double berth cannot be used as a double berth since the people in it would end up in a tangled heap not of their own making. Other settee berths are fine if they are to leeward, but those to windward (or any of them if the boat is

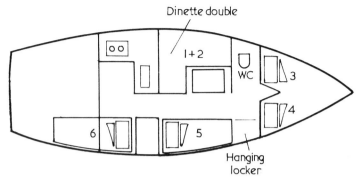

A common layout for a cruising boat offering six berths when in harbour. At sea it is a different story. Berths 1 & 2 could possibly be used as one berth if it is either to leeward or has a leecloth fitted; berths 3 & 4 would probably be untenable in a seaway; berth 5 could be used if it were to leeward or fitted with a leecloth; berth 6 should be usable at all times. Thus it is possible that there will be only three of the original six berths usable at sea

rolling a lot), must be fitted with leecloths to retain their occupants.

For all these reasons, if you are intending to make overnight or longer passages, study the accommodation plans and consider how many of the berths will actually be usable at sea. Those that are usable—it may be no more than 50 per cent—should be fitted with leecloths, but few builders provide these. A leecloth is simply a triangle, or better a rectangle, of stout cloth with one edge screwed down under the inboard edge of the berth cushion and the other corner or edge secured to the deckhead with lanyards. The cloth then holds the sleeper in place if he slides or rolls against it.

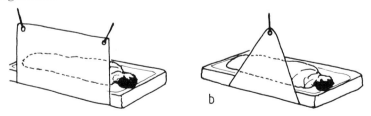

Rectangular leecloth (a) provides better security and support than triangular cloth (b)

60

The very simple accommodation of the First 18 Micro Cupper. Under Micro Cup rules there must be basic accommodation so that the boats can be trailed to meetings and then lived aboard by the crew. The lifting keel of the First 18 houses in the box in the centre of the cabin

DINETTE/DOUBLE BERTHS

Where a dinette arrangement is used in the main saloon it is usual to build it in such a way that it can be converted at night into a double berth. This is usually done by lowering the table to berth level and covering it with made-to-measure cushions. Such an arrangement only provides a narrow double berth, but at least it is just about adequate.

One or two things need consideration about dinette/double berths: first, there is going to be one less sea berth than harbour berths; second, is it going to be inconvenient to have to keep changing from one configuration to the other? third, investigate the stowage, when not in use, of the extra cushions required. The first point may not matter as someone will always be on watch, but if too many other berths will also be unusable

61

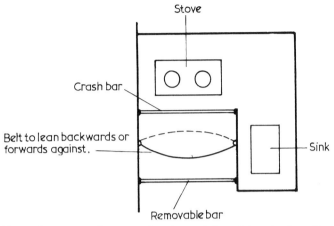

Alternative systems for protecting the cook from injury in the galley. Either a belt can be provided to lean backwards or forwards against, or a crash bar can be fitted across the front of the stove space with a removable bar to lean back on

for one reason or another, then the loss of one more berth could be a problem. How convenient swapping from dinette to double berth and back again will be depends largely on design. If the table simply slides down on a pillar and rests on the edges of a U-shaped settee or of two facing seats, then it should not be too awkward, but if it involves collapsing legs and folding arms it could be a problem. The stowage of cushions should also be something the designer has solved. Sometimes the backrests of the settee remove and fit on the lowered table which is straightforward, but occasionally you find that they have to be shoved down a quarter berth or left in the forecabin when they are not in use and that is not satisfactory at all.

QUARTER BERTHS

Quarter berths are not quarter size berths, but literally berths placed in the boat's quarters to port and starboard. In a boat with the cockpit abaft the accommodation, the quarter berths will run aft under the sidedecks and cockpit seats with only their heads in the cabin.

The Jaguar 21 lifting keel cruiser racer is one of a number of designs offering simple accommodation for four people and good club racing performance. The sailing picture shows her threequarter rig and powerful spinnaker (with an unfortunately tangled genoa about to be handed), while the interior shot (p 64) gives an idea of her accommodation. There are two berths forward, a galley amidships to port with one end against the keel box and two settee berths

As sea berths they are excellent being in a position of moderate motion and providing complete security on either tack, but they, or rather their occupants, do suffer the big drawback of being in direct line for any spray or rain coming through the open hatch. In the leeward bunk too you can easily be trodden on by a crewman stumbling through the hatchway.

Normally on fully crewed boats these berths are reserved for skipper and navigator as both can then be called easily and can get on deck quickly.

One very important design feature of quarter berths is the tunnel height, particularly at hips and/or shoulders. There is nothing worse than trying to sleep in a bunk you can't turn over in. If you get the chance, climb into the quarter berth on any 'possible' boat and try turning over.

BERTH CUSHIONS

The cushions used as bunk mattresses are made of foam plastic and are usually 3–4in deep. They can be covered either in cloth or PVC. Cloth is the favoured material as it can be coloured and patterned, forming part of the overall decor of the accommodation. It is also more comfortable to sit and lie on, but it does make it rather easy for the foam material to become wet with salt water and once a salt deposit is formed the cushions will never really be dry again. This fact makes it important to remove oilskins before sitting down.

The galley

The galley on a small boat is inevitably something of a compromise in terms of allowable space and facilities. Larger boats may be able to have twin sinks, iceboxes and pressurized hot and cold water, but the cooks on smaller boats have to cope with inadequate work surfaces, sinks that are too shallow or too small, with hand-pumped water and cookers offering just a couple of burners and a grill. Despite that, much thought goes into the designing of the galley as it is clearly important on a family boat to be able to produce appetising and adequate meals even if they are not as complex in preparation as they might be ashore.

What is essential in a seagoing galley is security for the cook and places to put hot dishes down where they will remain. The cook cannot easily keep one hand free for holding on so he or she must be able to wedge himself or herself against something. For that reason there is much to be said in favour of a U-shaped galley with a removable bar or strap across the open end. Alternatively a belt that can be hooked onto a secure point provides good protection against the cook being thrown *away* from his work, but don't forget the equally important matter of guarding against his being thrown *on to* the cooker. To prevent that happening a bar should be installed across the front of the cooker space, positioned so that the stove can still swing freely in its gimbals.

Although it is desirable on a monohulled boat at sea to have a gimballed cooker so that pots and pans stay on the stove and remain filled, in harbour it is often a nuisance. The ideal arrangement is a gimballed stove that can be fixed for harbour use either

65

A large galley like this provides lots of working space and large lockers, but it is very easy for the cook to be thrown about as the boat rolls or pitches. Ideally there would be a crash bar across the front of the cooker, a belt or strap for the cook to lean against and moveable fiddles on the work surfaces

by something like a bolt or by lifting the stove off its gimbals to stand on its own feet.

When comparing the galleys on various boats, also note where stowage is provided. All too often there is a deep, top-opening locker (frequently made into an icebox) situated in a corner. To reach down into it the cook has to lean over the stove and virtually up-end himself. Things required during cooking should, if possible, not be stowed outboard of the cooker as again they have to be reached across the hot stove.

On small boats it can be a great help to the cook if provision is made for him to sit and cook. This makes him a good deal more secure and if there is not full standing headroom at the stove it will save a lot of backache. If this is to be done, however, the stove and work surfaces must be low enough to work at easily.

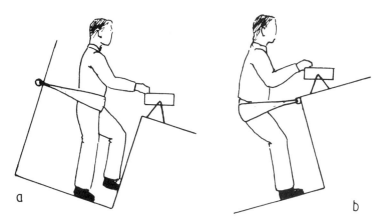

Use of cook's belt when working at stove on either tack

GAS FOR COOKING

Just as there is discussion and argument about the merits and dangers of diesel and petrol for engines, so there is about gas as a fuel for cooking on a boat. Many people argue strongly in favour of paraffin (kerosene), alcohol or even electricity, but the fact remains that the majority of boats are fitted with bottled butane or propane gas. It is convenient and clean to use despite the habit bottles have of running out half-way through the preparation of a meal.

The important thing to remember with gas is that it is heavier than air and will therefore sink into the bilges, where it may build up to explosive proportions, *if it is allowed to*. That is the key to the whole business. Don't allow gas to escape and you won't have trouble.

The bottles of gas should be stored in lockers that drain overboard thus preventing any seepage there from entering the boat. Piping should be well-secured copper with proper through-bulkhead fittings until close to the stove when it should be connected to certified flexible hose. Either this hose should also be used between bottle and copper piping or there should be a downward spiral of copper to the pressure regulator on top of the bottle.

Every time the gas is used it should be turned off afterwards at the bottle and consequently it is best to install the gas locker within reach of the main hatchway; otherwise, if it is cold or wet out no-one will bother to go on deck to turn the gas off. A subsidiary gas tap by the stove at the end of the copper piping is also a wise fitting, but it should not be used as a substitute for turning off at the bottle, rather as an additional precaution.

The toilet

Privacy is very hard to achieve on a small boat and nowhere more so than in the heads. Even if it can be shut off from the rest of the boat when in use, the toilet is much more a part of the living space than it is in a house, and people have to adjust to that fact.

Fitting a toilet between the vee berths in the forecabin is not a good idea as it means those berths cannot be used while the toilet is in use. The more usual arrangement is to have a separate compartment between the saloon and forecabin, generally with a hanging locker opposite. This section of the boat can then be closed off from the accommodation by doors to the forecabin and saloon. Alternatively there may be a separate compartment provided immediately inside the cabin to one side of the companionway. This site offers more room and use of the toilet does not interfere with the rest of the accommodation in any way, whereas with it sited between the saloon and forecabin it is usually necessary to close the fore and aft passage.

Whether a sea toilet evacuating directly into the sea, a chemical toilet with a holding tank fitted in the bilges or one incorporating a tank in the toilet itself, is chosen may depend on personal preference or outside regulations. Some areas do not permit the pumping of untreated effluent directly into the water, notably on the inland waterways, and in such places it is necessary to check that whatever boat you are interested in can comply with the regulations for holding tanks.

Although this toilet compartment is quite small there is storage space in the lockers behind and to the left of the toilet while a handbasin slides out over it. The seacocks are readily accessible for turning off after use

Tables

CHART TABLES

On a small boat it is nearly impossible to provide a permanent chart table—there simply is not enough room. The best that can be done is to offer a cabin table of adequate proportions or else a fold-out chart table. Where such tables fold or slide out from depends on the layout of the boat in question, but possible sites are over the head of one quarter berth or on a saloon bulkhead. Alternatively a removable cabin table may be set up over one

The Foxterrier 22 is another boat offering good sailing performance coupled with a very habitable interior. The feet of the settee berths extend forward through the mast bulkhead into the forecabin which is used as a big toilet compartment. By putting the toilet there on its own and doing away with the usual forward vee berths and convertible dinette/double berth in the saloon, the Foxterrier offers four practical sea berths at all times

saloon settee berth for use as a chart table.

Ideally a chart table will be large enough to set out an unfolded Admiralty chart, but that is asking a lot and will only be possible on the largest boats. At a more realistic level one has to aim for space enough to take a folded Admiralty chart which is about half the size of an unfolded one.

Not only must there be room to lay the chart out, there must be room also to work on all parts of the table. Having a shelf or other obstruction so low that you cannot work beneath it is always a nuisance as the chart has to be moved over until space is found. Another unsatisfactory arrangement is where the galley is covered over for use as a chart table. In the first place it means that the sink and cooker cannot be used while the chart table is needed, in the second the water pump will almost certainly drip on the chart and finally, as you work on the chart you will either move your parallel rules over a hump or hollow and get out of line, or your pencil will stab a hole in the chart as its point disappears down a crack between two of the galley covers.

This last is a point to look out for on all potential chart tables— if there is a hinge anywhere it should be fitted so that the gap between the two surfaces is as small as possible and the hinge itself is flush with the surfaces.

Where a permanent chart table is provided it is often at the head of a quarter berth with the berth used as a navigator's seat, allowing him to sit and work at the table. In that case the navigator's berth must be the quarter berth, else some other poor person is going to get sat upon.

I must confess to a preference for chart tables that you stand up to work at because they are usually larger as the space that would otherwise be needed for a seat can be covered by the table. I also find that when in pilotage waters the navigator comes below to look at the chart, often in oilskins, dripping wet, and he naturally stands at the chart table rather than sitting down and making the seat or his bedding wet.

Chart stowage must also be considered. Rolling charts is extremely bad practice for the simple reason that they will never again lie flat on a chart table. With a permanent table the surface is usually hinged to form the lid of a shallow box and charts are stowed in that, but where no permanent table exists it is important to consider what you will do with the charts. A few can be stowed beneath berth cushions (in which case the occupant has to be disturbed when a new chart is required), but it is more satisfactory if stowage can be incorporated in a fold-away chart table or in the saloon table. There is no reason why a cabin table should not be built as a box in which the folded charts can be kept. There is no perfect solution, but when comparing various boats it is an important point to check.

CABIN TABLES

A cabin table is not just something to eat off. It can be a coffee table to lounge round and yarn into the night; it can be a centre for children to do jigsaws, paint or read at; it can be a card or Scrabble table on wet days in port; as already discussed, it can be a chart table; it can also be part of a double berth.

Tables can be permanent, folding, gimballed, sliding, extending, hanging. They can have fiddles to stop things sliding off. They should not block fore and aft movement through the boat and they should be strong, for certainly someone will grab them or fall against them when the boat lurches unexpectedly. They can be a blessing or a nuisance, but on even the smallest boat they should be there, somewhere.

Headroom

You cannot expect a small boat to provide full standing headroom, indeed it is only on fairly large boats that it can be achieved throughout the accommodation. A tall person will find it even more rarely.

With or without standing headroom, good sitting headroom with comfortable backrests is most important. If this is not provided you will never be comfortable and it is surprising how

72

many boats you come across where the headroom is adequate but there is nothing to lean back against. On a small boat a shelf at the right height and width will not only be useful, but will provide a backrest too. Without it when you do lean back the corner of the sidedeck gets you in the back of the neck.

People with any sort of back trouble must consider headroom very seriously. If there is 'standing headroom under the main hatch' there is a little bit less elsewhere, which means you go round in a semi-stooped posture and that will bring out any latent backaches. It is better for those people either to go for a boat with full standing headroom (for them) throughout or to choose one with good, comfortable sitting headroom, in which case they come below and sit down straight away.

What exactly a builder means when he says his boat has full standing headroom is open to wide interpretation and it is best to ask for exact measurements in the saloon (not just under the hatch) and in other parts of the boat such as forecabin and toilet. Otherwise see the boat and try walking round down below.

Lockers and storage space

There are never enough lockers on a boat. No matter how much clever use is made of available space, you will always manage to fill it and wish for more, so what there is must be well planned and well used.

Each crew member should be allocated a private locker in which to keep his or her clothes and personal items, together with space in a hanging locker if required. This hanging locker should be for dry clothing only, oilskins being kept separately in a 'wet' locker that drains into the bilges. If possible this locker should be near the main hatch so that crew members come below, take off their oilskins and hang them up straight away without dripping all over the rest of the accommodation. It is useful also to have a vent into it from the engine compartment so that when the engine is running warm air can be allowed into the locker to dry whatever is there.

73

The space under bunks is obvious storage space, but the top access generally provided has the drawback that if something is wanted from the locker under an occupied berth the sleeper has to be woken up and turned out. Front access, however, does not always make getting things in and out very easy, so perhaps the best arrangement is to have both top and front access.

Cave lockers, that is open-fronted lockers without doors, are very useful in cockpits for stowing winch handles, sail tiers and so on, but do have the disadvantage of being able to spill their contents as readily as they accept them in the first place. For this reason they are not too good an idea down below.

Food lockers need big entrances and shelves with high lips (fiddles) along the open edge to stop the contents shooting out when the door of the windward one is opened. Sliding fronts of clear plastic on lockers under the side decks are good as they let you see exactly what is in the locker before you open it.

All lockers require ventilation. The easiest way to provide this is by having openings top and bottom or louvred doors. Few lockers are thus provided, but if something is not done the contents will grow mildew, or in the case of fresh food will simply rot.

Lighting

Most new boats are fitted with interior electric lights, particularly if an inboard engine is installed as battery charging is then easy. Where an outboard engine is provided it may be that cabin lights are an optional extra (see Chapter 4).

The alternative to electric lighting is the use of paraffin (kerosene) lamps or dry cell lights. Paraffin lamps give a cosy glow that has a definite charm but is not too easy to read by; I have always found it necessary to have more than one lit, even in a small cabin with white-painted deckhead and bulkheads. Dry cell lights on the other hand are simple to install and use, and the batteries shouldn't need changing more than once or twice a season (depending on amount of use).

Two modern cruiser racers sailing in company. On the left is a Comfort 30 and on the right a Carter 30 under spinnaker and with a permanently mounted radar reflector at the masthead. Despite having the same overall length, these boats are quite different in external appearance and arrangement below decks. Both boats, however, are typical of their breed, being strong, fast, good seagoing craft

Discharge tube strip lights use far less current than conventional festoon bulb lights but they can cause interference on electronic instruments such as radio direction finders. It is perhaps best to have both types of light available so that the main strip lighting can be turned off when an RDF set is in use and smaller bulb lights put on. If these are over each berth they also provide individual reading lights which won't disturb the rest of an off-watch crew.

Ventilation

Few production boats have sufficient ventilators and none has too many. Wooden boats were often far better provided with ventilation than today's glassfibre ones because the builders realized that a vessel with poor air circulation was open to attack by rot and mildew. Glassfibre boats won't rot, but their contents can still grow mildew, they can still be damp and musty and unpleasant odours can still be trapped within the accommodation.

What is often forgotten is that the natural flow of air through a boat is from aft forward, not the other way. Vents must be arranged so that air can not only enter the boat, it can also leave her. It must be able to get into and out of lockers, particularly food and clothes lockers. Where wooden boats normally had a ceiling of slats fastened to the inside of the ribs, allowing free circulation of air, GRP boats often have a lining material stuck directly to the hull or have a complete interior moulding, neither of which allows air to circulate freely.

Many boats are provided with no more than a token pair of vents, one over the galley and one over the heads compartment. That is not enough; there must be a designed system of vents to introduce fresh air and extract stale air. The main and fore hatches should not be included in the system, they should be additional ventilators as a boat must still be properly ventilated when left closed up on her moorings. However, to assist ventilation when occupied, it is better to have an aft-opening forehatch (that is with the hinge along its forward edge) as it can then be left open at anchor without rain blowing in when the boat lies head to wind. If it opens forwards it will usually have to be closed. Also, the after cabin bulkhead, at the mainhatch, should not slope forwards, because even with the hatch closed, rain can still fall straight into the cabin if the fashion boards are not dropped in to close the opening, and that is not always desirable or possible.

Ventilation of the engine space is important too, especially with an inboard petrol engine. Where such an engine is used it may be advisable to have spark-proof electric extractor fans installed to remove any build-up of fumes before starting the engine.

Heating

You are unlikely to find a boat with heating fitted as part of the standard specification unless you are looking at very expensive craft, but some secondhand boats are equipped with heaters. The kinds of heater most widely used include warm air, gas catalytic heaters, solid fuel and pressurized paraffin stoves.

Warm air heaters are probably best suited to motor boats and motor sailers where larger sources of electrical power are available and bigger supplies of diesel can be carried. Catalytic heaters are both powerful and safe and can be installed on even the smallest of boats, while a solid fuel stove, being rather heavy if not bulky, can best be installed on a larger displacement motor boat, canal boat or heavy displacement cruising yacht. Pressurised paraffin stoves can be fitted on any medium-to-large boat.

Whichever kind of heater is fitted, it is a real luxury in cold weather to come off watch and warm yourself before a hot stove. They are useful too for drying wet clothing.

Colours

More attention is paid to colour on boats than it used to be. Where once a boat was of one colour on the topsides and had berth cushions of a sober hue, it is common now for multicoloured paint jobs on the topsides, often incorporating the boat's name, and patterned, bright materials covering the berth cushions. When comparing possible boats it is worth investigating what colours are used to see if you like them. On production boats there are normally two or three hull colours available with others at additional cost, but interior decor is usually unalterable.

If you intend using the boat in areas of intense sunshine beware of decks that are white – the sun on them will hurt your eyes. Better to insist on a pale colour such as blue, grey or cream.

Tinted windows

Tinted materials are widely used for boat windows and they are a mixed blessing. They reduce the light in the cabin which helps an off-watch crew to sleep during the day and they make it harder for people to look in when the boat is moored alongside, but on the other hand they make a bright sunny sky look ominous and stormy and curtains are still required when moored for the night in a marina.

What is really useful is a forehatch or mainhatch of tinted plastic, as they let a lot of additional light into the accommodation without having to be open. They also maintain a degree of privacy that would be lost with uncoloured transparent hatches.

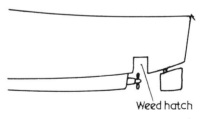

Weed hatch

Weed hatch for access to fouled propeller

Weed hatches

Any boat intended for use on inland waterways with a propeller under the stern, that is one that can not be lifted like an outboard or outdrive leg, should have a weed hatch. This is simply a chamber in the bottom of the boat over the propeller with a removable cover allowing the crew to reach down with their hands and clear weed, plastic bags or other debris from around the propeller. The lid must of course be above the waterline and should have a good seal on it.

4 IS THAT AN EXTRA?

In the first chapter of this book I warned that when considering buying a boat you must give serious thought to how much you can afford to pay, having regard to the fact that the actual purchase price of the boat is only part of the overall cost of boating. I mentioned too that buying a new boat always means buying equipment not supplied with her by the builder—equipment not in her 'standard inventory'. It is true also that with a second-hand boat you are unlikely to buy one which is completely equipped and will have to add certain extra pieces of gear and equipment.

Another item to beware of is VAT which is often omitted from quoted prices for supplying and fitting equipment. This adds a substantial amount to the bill and may make it cheaper to buy the bits and pieces elsewhere and fit them yourself. In this way you will at least avoid the cost of labour and the VAT on it, but against this must be balanced the price you have to pay for equipment as opposed to the price the builder has to pay for the same item.

While one boat may at first appear far cheaper than another, it is only after careful study of the builders' literature to see what is included (or more important what is omitted) at the quoted price that you will be able to make a fair comparison of the two craft. What you need to do is make a list for each boat of what items are included in the standard basic price and what ones will have to be added as extras. These must then be priced up and the total added to the boat's basic price, at which stage you can accurately compare the total prices of the boats. The result may well

An International 470 dinghy leading an International 505 with both crews out on their trapezes. Both are very sophisticated racing dinghies and the 470 is one of the classes raced in the Olympic Games. The mast of this one is bowed to flatten the mainsail and improve its driving power in the prevailing conditions

be a reversal of the first impression. It is also interesting to compare the prices quoted in the builder's 'extras' list with your own prices for buying and fitting the various items to see which is cheaper.

The lists of gear and equipment which follow cover a variety of types of boat and a wide range of levels of use, but they will act as a guide to the equipment likely to be needed.

Sailing cruisers and motor sailers

Sails: at least mainsail, genoa,
    working jib and storm jib;
    extra sails such as spinnaker
    and its gear
Engine and controls   Compass
Fuel and water tanks   Anchor and cable

81

Kedge and warp
Pulpit, pushpit and
    guardrails
Mooring warps
Fenders—minimum of four
Boat-hook
Lifebuoys and lights
Lifejackets
Lifeharnesses
Liferaft
Echo-sounder
Electrics and electronics
    (wind and sailing
    instruments)
Navigation lights
Radar reflector
Fire extinguishers
Flares
Foghorn
Bilge pump
First aid kit
Emergency tiller
Riding light
Log
RDF
Handbearing compass

Navigation instruments
    (dividers, parallel rules, etc)
Charts
Pilot books
Barometer
Binoculars
Boarding ladder
Ventilators
Interior lights
Toilet
Cooker
Gas bottles (or other cooking
    fuels)
Bedding—sleeping bags,
    pillows, cushions
Crockery
Cutlery
Pots and pans
Oilskins
Boots
Sprayhood
Anchor ball and
    motorsailing cone
Tender
Radar

Motor cruisers and canal cruisers

(Items marked * do not apply to motor cruisers and those
marked † do not apply to canal cruisers.)

Engine and controls
Fuel and water tanks
Compass †
Anchor and cable †
Kedge and warp †

Pulpit, pushpit and
    guardrails†
Mooring warps
Fenders
Boat hook

Lifebuoys and lights
Lifejackets
Lifeharnesses
Liferaft †
Echo-sounder†
Electrics and electronics
   (including engine
   instruments)
Navigation lights †
Radar reflector †
Fire extinguishers †
Flares †
Fog horn
Bilge pump
First aid kit
Emergency tiller
Riding light †
Log †
RDF †
Handbearing compass †
Navigation instruments
   (dividers, parallel rules,
   etc)†
Charts (waterways guides)

Barometer †
Binoculars
Boarding ladder †
Ventilators
Interior lights
Toilet
Cooker
Gas bottles (or other cooking
   fuels)
Bedding—sleeping bags,
   cushions, pillows
Crockery
Cutlery
Pots and pans
Oilskins
Boots
Tender †
Radar †
Weedhatch *
Lock windlass *
Mooring stakes and hammer*
Auxiliary outboard motor for
   single-engine motor boats

Sportsboats

Engine and controls
Fuel tanks
Instruments (rev counter/
   speedometer, engine
   instruments)
Anchor and warp
Fenders
Warps
Paddles

Bailer
Navigation lights
Lifejackets
Flares
Wet suits
Water-skis
Tow-rope
Trailer and lighting board
Boat and engine covers

Racing dinghies

Sails and spinnaker to class
  rules
Self-bailers
Paddles
Anchor and warp
Painter
Buoyancy bags
Measurement certificate
Lifejackets

Oilskins
Wet suits
Boots
Gloves
Trailer
Launching trolley and
  lighting board
Boat cover

5 CONSIDERING GEAR AND EQUIPMENT

Sails and sailmakers

The sails supplied with a normal production boat will have been made as part of a bulk order placed by the builder and the sail-maker will probably be the one that quoted the best price for making them. That is not meant to imply that they will necess-arily be of poor quality or poor cut, but it is true to say that they will not be of the best possible shape or of the most sophisticated cloth. For these things you have to pay dearly.

If your main purpose is to race the boat and you are going to go all out to win, then it will be worth your while going either to the maker of the standard sails or to another loft of your choice and asking them to make you a suit of sails specially for your boat. These will include many more sails than the mainsail and No 2 genoa normally supplied with a production boat and will be tailor-made with re-cutting and re-shaping carried out if they are not quite right first time. It may even entail a day out with the sailmaker on board so that he can see exactly how they set and what the problems are.

For those whose intentions are simply to cruise with the family the standard suit of sails plus a few extra ones, such as storm jib and light genoa, will be perfectly adequate. Although there is no reason why the family man should accept sails that will produce significantly inferior performance, he is not going after that last fraction of a knot that may make all the difference in racing. He is more concerned with long life for his sails, which

These three dinghies have just rounded a buoy during a handicap race and are bunched together. Racing like this requires complete concentration, any lapse being paid for in lost places, and it provides competitors with a great deal of excitement

means they must be well reinforced at all stress and chafe points and may be of a slightly heavier cloth with less filler in it than would be used for a racing suit. The filler used in many racing sails helps to make them a little stiffer so that they maintain a good aerofoil shape; unfortunately it gradually falls out with use and certainly with being stuffed into sail bags rather than folded and packed carefully.

Exactly what sails you choose to carry depends on the boat and your pocket, but the basic wardrobe for a sloop should be mainsail, genoa, working jib and storm jib. With a modern masthead rigged boat these sails may be described as mainsail, No 1, No 2 and No 3 genoas. In addition you might decide to carry a spinnaker, but there is little need for any other sails. One variation on this wardrobe might be to have a roller-reefing headsail with a separate storm jib and possibly a light reaching genoa. For racing, on the other hand, you could easily be in the market for up to five different genoas plus at least one spinnaker and a blooper besides the mainsail.

The boatbuilder's list of optional extras may include the additional sails you want and the easiest thing is to buy them from him, but it could prove cheaper to go direct to a sail loft with your order. This may not be the case if the builder is obtaining a price reduction for bulk ordering, but it is worth checking.

Spars

As with the sails, the builder will supply mast and boom as part of the standard specification and is likely to offer a spinnaker pole and gear as an optional extra. Unless you are intending to use the boat for a specialised purpose, such as long-term ocean cruising, you are unlikely to want to do anything other than accept the spars provided. It is only if you feel that for your purposes you should step a mast of rather heavier section than the standard one, or if you want a boom with internal slab-reefing pennants rather than the standard roller-reefing gear, that you need to try to negotiate a price ex-spars and buy them elsewhere.

Even when buying a kit boat or bare hull it is generally best to buy the spars from the builder as he can obtain a reduction from the spar maker for ordering several identical sets at the same time. If the builder is not able to do this for any reason then it is necessary to go direct to the spar maker of your choice—or more probably to several to obtain quotations before deciding on one firm. Alternatively you can buy aluminium alloy extrusions of the right dimensions and put the fittings on yourself. There are a few spar firms that actually sell mast and boom kits which, with care and a good pop rivetter, are not too hard to put together. Naturally there should be some saving in cost by doing this. One point to watch though is that if internal halyards are to be used (see next section) then the mast must be sound-deadened or they will make an unbearable din as they slap back and forth. The sound-deadening is usually achieved by lining the spar with expanded polystyrene foam.

There are not many people today who opt for a wooden mast since they are rather heavier than aluminium ones and more expensive. Still, if you are a good carpenter and have the length of bench required, there is no reason why you should not build your own spars, particularly the boom or spinnaker and running poles. Modern glues help to make very strong scarfs and the use of power tools for shaping and preparing the wood lightens the work. You would be well advised though, before starting on the job, to seek the advice of the boat's designer concerning dimensions for the spars.

Rigging

The standing rigging provided with a new boat is most probably made of stainless steel, either in the form of 1 × 19 strand or 7 × 7 or 7 × 19 wire rope. Strand is made up of nineteen wires twisted together in one long spiral which is stiff and relatively smooth, whereas wire rope is lumpy to the touch in the same way that ordinary three-strand laid rope is. It is made up of six bunches of either seven or nineteen wires which are first twisted together then formed into a spiral around a central heart which consists of seven or nineteen wires running in parallel (untwisted). The diagrams should make this a little clearer.

Size for size, measured as the diameter of the total structure 1 × 19 strand is stronger than wire rope and can therefore be used in a slightly smaller size for a given job such as standing rigging. This means a small reduction in weight aloft, which is always helpful in reducing the boat's tendency to heel, and being smoother, creates less windage. It is, however, very stiff and can be damaged by bending too tightly. It therefore requires special terminals for connecting it to both mast and rigging screws and it cannot be used for such things as halyards.

As the ends of 1 × 19 strand cannot be connected to the mast or the rigging screws by forming it into an eye round a thimble then using pins or shackles, special terminals have been devised. These take the form of 'roll swaged' and Norseman or Sta-Lok

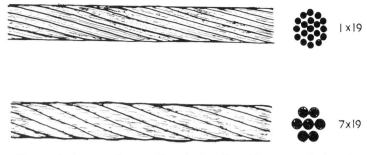

Types of wire rope for standing rigging (1 × 19 construction) and running rigging (7 × 19)

swageless terminals. The former consist of stainless-steel tubes (swages) which are slipped over the wire and then crushed onto it under extremely high pressure. The free end of the tube is made as either a flat eye, T-ball or a fork for fitting to the bottle-screws or mast tangs. Norseman and Sta-Lok terminals also end in a flat eye but are put on using spanners and other simple tools rather than costly swageing machines—in other words they can be fitted by the careful amateur. In essence a cone of metal is pushed into the ends of the wire and a clamping cover with a flat eye at the end is screwed down over it.

Many boats, particularly older secondhand ones or those fitted out by cost-conscious home builders, have galvanised wire standing rigging. Size for size it is not quite as strong as stainless steel and it requires more maintenance to prevent it from rusting, but it has the advantage over stainless 1 × 19 (as does stainless wire rope) of being flexible, so that it can be formed into an eye round a thimble.

At each end of a piece of stainless or galvanised wire-rope standing-rigging an eye can be put in allowing it to be fastened with a pin or shackle to the mast tang or rigging screw. The eye and thimble can be put in either by hand splicing or Talurit (Nicopress) splicing. The former, as in eyesplicing rope, is done by weaving the strands of the end in a regular pattern over and under the strands of the standing part. Talurit or Nicopress splicing, on the other hand, is somewhat similar to swageing in

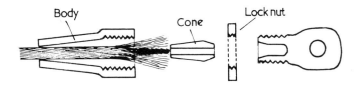

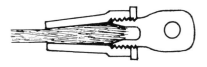

A swageless terminal for 1 × 19 construction standing rigging

that a machine is required. However, the machine is simpler and less expensive so most rigging shops and sailmakers have one. To do such a splice the wire is bent round a thimble of the required size and the end of the wire is bound to the standing part by a compressed metal band; copper for stainless steel wire and aluminium for galvanized wire. It's a very quick and simple process.

One or two things to keep an eye out for with standing rigging: signs of the wire pulling out of a badly fitted swageless terminal (Norseman or Sta-Lok); broken strands at the top of swages or Talurit bands; a distinct bend or kink where wire enters a swage; incorrect material used for Talurit bands; rusting of galvanized wire at the crowns of thimbles; water trapped under the servings of hand splices. All of these smack of poor fitting originally and inadequate maintenance subsequently. If any such condition is found, suspect the rigging until it can be checked and approved by a rigger or surveyor. Particularly beware of any broken wires.

Finally, all standing rigging moves, fore and aft and athwart-ships. To accommodate that movement it is essential to fit some form of 'universal joint' between the rigging screws and chain-plates. If stainless-steel loops are used instead of chainplates these may suffice, but otherwise jointed 'toggles' must be installed. Often they are omitted as an economy, but it's a false one and something, even just a shackle, must be put in to allow movement in all directions.

Where once halyards were rigged so that they ran outside the mast, it is now common practice for them to be rigged internally, in which case it is essential to have a sound-deadened spar or their noise will soon drive you mad. The idea of internal halyards comes from racing boats concerned with all possible reduction of windage aloft and while they do achieve this they make reeving off replacement halyards awkward and watching for chafe also much harder. The alternative, externally rigged halyards, makes it much easier to spot wear in good time and for a pure cruising boat may well be preferred.

In the same way that there is a choice between internal and external halyards, so there is a choice between all-rope ones, all-wire ones and combination wire-and-rope ones. In most instances you will accept whatever the boat arrives with, but where you have a choice there are various pros and cons to be considered for each type.

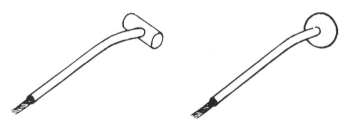

T-ball terminals for connecting standing rigging to mast. Used with 1 × 19 strand

All-rope halyards are either made of three-strand laid rope or a plaited line. They are easy to handle, can be hand spliced simply and old ones are always useful for lashing odd things down. Against them is the fact that they stretch more than wire, although it is now possible to use Kevlar carbon-fibre halyards which have stretch characteristics very similar to those of wire. Rope also creates more windage and can chafe more readily (but

The halyards on this boat are led aft on the coachroof to a pair of winches: a conventional two speed winch on the left and a self-tailing type on the right with the halyard wound round the barrel, over the stripper and up into the revolving cleat. Note that the three halyards are led through 'stoppers' ahead of the winches. Each halyard is set up hard, with the aid of the winch, the stopper is then engaged to hold the tension and the line is taken off the winch, freeing it for use with another halyard

92

does not wear out sheaves as fast as wire does).

All-wire halyards are strong, light and create little windage. Unfortunately they must be wound on to an enclosed drum as they cannot be handled and this is the cause of a lot of trouble, even injury as fingers can be trapped while trying to sort the turns out on the barrel. Many people find them perfectly satisfactory, but in my experience they are not to be recommended.

Wire-and-rope halyards try to achieve the best of both worlds by using the wire to reduce stretch and windage while leaving the rope tail for comfortable handling. The rope to wire splice is not too complicated but must be done carefully and inspected frequently. Only the rope must be turned up on a cleat, the wire must always be confined to the winch barrel. The wire must be a rope (that is to say flexible) not strand, such as is used for standing rigging, and it must be checked for crippled or broken wires frequently. The masthead sheaves will also require at least annual inspection for wear.

On a small boat which doesn't need halyard winches I think it is best to use all-rope halyards, but where winches are required the choice is open.

Winches

Even quite small production yachts are equipped with at least a pair of headsail sheet winches if not halyard winches too. Larger boats are either fitted with spinnaker sheet winches as well or the builders offer them as part of the optional spinnaker gear package. On a small boat winches may be a bit of a luxury, but sheeting in a sail of any size when it is full and drawing is undeniably hard work especially for a lightweight family crew, so they are not to be sneezed at.

Boats of about 25ft and upwards will probably have two-speed winches: the high speed for bringing in the slack sheet and as much of the rest as possible, then the low speed for grinding in and fine trim. This allows the person working the winch to operate it with one hand leaving the other to haul on the tail of the sheet so that tension is maintained and the sheet does not slip on the barrel. Life can be made even easier by fitting 'self-tailing' winches. These have a revolving cleat on top which holds the tail of the sheet and leads it off the barrel in a continuous process. The person winching can then apply both hands to the handle or have one to hold on with. As self-tailing winches are more expensive than ordinary ones they are not often fitted as standard.

No precise statements can be made about what size of sail requires sheet and halyard winches, but if you are building a boat of more than about 20ft you would be wise to fit them if at all possible financially as they are of great assistance. It will soon put an unsure crew off if they cannot set a halyard up hard or sheet a headsail in easily. They will begin to feel they can't cope and that the boat is too big when in reality they could handle one half as big again if she were properly equipped.

Some winches have their handle at the bottom of the barrel while others have one fitting into a central hole on top of the barrel. Many of the bottom-action winches have fixed (captive) handles and this can be an advantage for halyards as the handle cannot then be dropped overboard and extra turns can be put on easily, but for sheet winches it is often a nuisance as the sheet invariably wraps itself round the handle when being let fly. Larger winches almost exclusively have top action with removable handles. These handles can be revolved through 360°, unlike the bottom-action handles which are operated like a ratchet, back and forth over a limited arc. Being able to revolve them completely makes operation faster, but means that the handle *must* be removed after use, otherwise, should anything go wrong, it will whip round and cause serious injury to anyone it hits.

Winch handles are costly items so it is worth buying handles which lock into the barrel socket to prevent them coming out unexpectedly, and providing stowage pockets near the winches.

Because of the very high loads imposed on sheet winches they must be well fastened down with bolts going through strong mounts and backing plates or pads. It is also important, although good builders will have made sure of it already, to check that the sheet or halyard has a fair lead onto the winch barrel otherwise nasty snarl-ups will occur.

Deck fittings

No matter what the kind of boat—motor cruiser, sailing dinghy, sportsboat or sailing cruiser—the deck fittings must be strong, of good design and properly secured. Far too many boats are equipped with poorly designed, undersized fittings. Some of the worst offenders are cleats and fairleads provided for mooring warps and anchor cables. Many of these have sharp angles which cut and chafe lines.

Not only must fittings be strong enough for the job, they must be securely fastened down, which generally means through-bolting to back-up pads or plates. These spread the load and reduce the chances of the fitting pulling out. They should also be in the right place. That sounds obvious and should be, but it is surprising how many boats have, for example, a mooring cleat in the middle of the foredeck and a central stemhead roller so that the anchor cable perpetually and unavoidably fouls the forestay. The whole problem could be solved by having an offset bow roller or better a pair of them—but apparently the builders and designers don't think of it.

Canal cruisers need fittings for tying fenders to as they seldom carry guardwires and the alternative fixing points are the coach-roof grabrails which result in a series of snares along the side-decks created by the pennants. Sportsboats intended for water-skiing need strong towing eyes or a pillar, the latter making driving easier and avoiding the ski line pulling across the outboard engine during tight turns. All boats need strong, secure grabrails—lots of them—with room between the rail and the surface they are fastened to for a complete hand grip. A finger hold is not enough, you must be able to clench your hand round them and move it through 180°, then if you are thrown off-balance your grip stands far more of a chance of remaining secure.

Ground tackle

Ground tackle, that is to say anchor and cable, is surprisingly not always included as standard equipment on a new boat and has to be purchased as an extra. Clearly, on a seagoing boat, this is a serious omission and it is encouraging that the majority of builders include at least a main anchor with a few fathoms of chain and 15 fathoms of warp. This is about the minimum one can get away with and should be added to at the earliest opportunity.

The ground tackle of even a small estuary and shoalwaters cruiser should include a main anchor (bower) and a kedge with at least 3 fathoms of chain and 20–30 fathoms of warp on each. If all-chain scope is used for the bower-anchor then 15 fathoms may be sufficient. Larger boats cruising deeper waters and going further afield will require proportionately larger anchors and maybe 5 fathoms of chain plus 50–60 fathoms of warp on each anchor, or 30 fathoms of chain with a 20-fathom warp on the bower and five of chain with thirty of warp on the kedge.

All of this will need to be stowed somewhere readily accessible and the anchor wells of some boats will not be large enough, so some system of leading the cable down to a locker beneath the well may be needed. Alternatively the older plan of stowing the anchor on deck and leading the cable down to a chain locker may be adopted. Where an anchor well is provided of large enough size it is convenient as it keeps the deck clear of one more obstruction, but check that the lid can be opened with the cable running between bow roller and cleat or samson-post. Sometimes the lid is trapped by the cable which doesn't help anyone. Remember also that the bitter end of the cable must be fastened so that it can be reached easily and that the anchor must be lashed down.

Warps and fenders

As with the ground tackle, where warps and fenders are provided by the builder it is likely that they will be a bare minimum. This is understandable, but may lead the new owner to think that he is all right for those items and can turn his attention to other matters. It is only when he comes to use them during a cruise that he finds himself short.

Particularly on motor boats with a lot of flare at the bows, it is essential to carry big fenders and in this case they need to be ball-shaped rather than the usual sausages. Otherwise you may need to lash several sausages together to form an adequate fender. For boats with near-upright topsides the sausage-shaped fenders are perfectly good and easier to stow, but there must be plenty of them, especially if you moor anywhere that someone else has to moor outside you. Then you will have to provide fenders on both sides to supplement those of the other boats.

As to warps, these must be long and strong. Don't choose the cheapest line available as you are entrusting your valuable boat to it and it is likely to be susceptible to chafe. Line of a better quality which is more resistant to chafe will last longer and may even work out cheaper in the end.

Chafe is a serious problem, especially if the fairleads have sharp edges and it is wise to carry anti-chafe gear. This can take the form of plastic tubing to be slipped over the line and tied or wedged into the fairlead, or it can be rags wrapped round the line. The tubing is better and more sightly.

Pulpits, pushpits and guardrails

Apart from small, fast motor boats and canal cruisers, it is most unusual to find a modern boat without at least a pulpit and guardrails if not a pushpit as well. Micro Tonners are some of the few without them, but for normal family use they are a useful 'safety fence' round the boat which helps retain crew members, particularly children, and also dowsed sails.

It must be remembered that the pulpits, pushpits and stanchions are all rather easily damaged when lying alongside either another boat or a harbour wall. While they are good at withstanding high loads trying to push them outwards, which is what they are designed to do, they are surprisingly weak if anything tries to

Two views of the Pegasus 800, a 26ft cruiser racer of sturdy construction and good sailing performance. A stainless steel boarding ladder is folded up on her stern to form part of the pushpit, but can be let down so that the lowest rung will be below water and thus of use to a person who has fallen overboard and is struggling to climb back on to the boat

push them inwards. Thus, if going ashore with a mooring line, don't try to fend the boat off the jetty or pontoon by pushing on the stanchions or wires. If alongside a wall as the tide rises keep checking that the rails don't hook under anything. Similarly when lying alongside another boat watch out for the two sets of stanchions and rails fouling each other as the boats move about on the wakes of passing craft.

When looking at a boat with a view to buying her, give the pulpit in particular a good tug to see how strong it is. Also consider how easy or otherwise it is going to be to pass the bower-anchor through it. Where there are two rails or two struts close together there may be a problem.

If there is a choice between having a single guardwire and twin wires it is probably better to take the pair as your chances of sliding under them are less than under a single wire. It's very easy to slip, fall on your back and slide across the deck, so you want it to be difficult to slide right under the wire.

It is essential to insulate the guardwires from the pulpit and pushpit otherwise they will interfere with the use of an RDF set. The easiest way to do this is with a lanyard-lashing between the wires and the pushpit. This method has the advantage that the lanyards can be cut and the guardwires dropped quickly if recovering a man overboard.

Electrics

It is an unfortunate fact that electrical installations do not like damp, salt-laden environments, so the electrics on a boat invariably get off to a bad start in life. Add to that the feeling of many people like me that electricity is some sort of magic—like engines—and wiring with the provision of an appropriate power source is something of a problem. We tend to rely on the good sense of the designer and boat builder to do things properly, but if building a boat ourselves we have to seek advice from experts.

The average boat requires electrical power first for starting her engine(s) then for interior and navigation lights (including compass light). Some power may be needed for electronic instruments, but most of these can be run on internal dry batteries. The engine is usually used to charge the batteries through an attached alternator and because of this it is necessary (unless hand starting is very easy) to have two separate batteries: one solely for starting the engine and one for all other purposes. Larger craft may need further batteries to give additional power, but for the average family boat this will be sufficient.

The batteries must be individually of large enough capacity for their job and there must be a means of tapping power from both of them at once for engine-starting in the event of a low or flat starting-circuit battery. You can't bump start a boat. There must also be a device ensuring even charging of each battery and you must make checking the acid level in them a regular routine, just as it is for your car.

It should be possible to uncover all of the electrical wiring in the boat so that additional wires can be put in or damaged ones replaced. If they are run through plastic conduit this won't be possible, but there should be a light line installed as a messenger through the conduit so that a new wire can be pulled through easily.

There seems to be some difference of opinion over the use of fuses or circuit breakers, but in practice I feel the circuit breakers are handier when their use is possible as they can be reset and spares need not be carried. With fuses you have to take along spares of each size.

Interior lights may either be common bulb types or gaseous discharge strip lights. The latter take less out of the battery once they are started, but they tend to interfere with the use of radio direction finders. Perhaps the ideal is to have a main cabin strip light with bulb lights at the chart table and by each berth so the occupant can read when off-watch at night without disturbing anyone else.

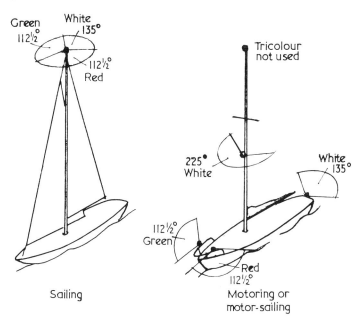

Navigation lights and their sectors of display required at night

Navigation lights must conform with the detailed require-ments laid down in the Regulations for Preventing Collisions at Sea. The advent of masthead tricolour lights for small craft which use only a single bulb has reduced battery drain consider-ably, but it must be remembered that a motor boat or a sailing boat under power (or motorsailing) cannot use the single tricol-

101

our. They must use port and starboard lights (though these may be a single bicolour lantern on smaller craft) with separate stern light and a white steaming light positioned at least one metre above the side lights. Thus on a sailing boat you may have a tri-colour light for use when sailing which does not create too much battery drain, but your batteries must also be big enough to cope with the high drain of all the separate lights. However, this is not quite as bad as it sounds since the engine will be charging the bat-teries all the time the extra lights are in use.

Bigger sailing boats or motor cruisers may carry a generator separate from the main engine and this is indeed useful as it will allow them to run power-tools requiring mains voltage besides alleviating the need to run the main engine daily (on a sailing cruiser at sea for a long time). It will probably be more efficient as a battery charger as well, but do not use it too much in harbour as you will annoy your near neighbours with the noise.

Electronics

In the same way that electrical installations do not like damp and salt, the first requirement of any electronic instrument installed on a boat is that it should be waterproof. If the instrument is not, or is only spray proof, then it should be made clear to you at the time of purchase so that you do not attempt to fit it in the open.

Most electronic instruments can be operated from internal dry-cell batteries, but some requiring more power must be run from the ship's supply. Using internal batteries reduces the required capacity for the ship's supply batteries and a failure of these batteries still allows the instrument to operate. There is also no chance of leaving an instrument on and unwittingly running the main battery flat.

ECHO-SOUNDERS

The first electronic instrument that most people select is an echo-sounder as it saves heaving and coiling a wet and often tangled lead line to find the depth of water. These instruments operate in principle by emitting a sound signal from a transducer in the bottom of the boat and timing the return of the signal as it bounces back off the seabed. The depth is then shown on a display usually taking the form of a dial with a needle, neon light, LED (Light Emitting Diode) indicator or digital readout, but some echo-sounders record a trace on paper giving a permanent record of the bottom contours. These are not generally used by yachtsmen but are useful to fishermen. Of the other displays, a flashing light gives the most information as its width indicates the hardness (or softness) of the bottom, hence giving an idea of its nature. A hard, rocky bottom shows as a crisp, narrow line while a soft ooze shows up as a wide, indistinct band of light.

The echo-sounder transducer may either be fitted into a hole cut through the hull, or with some hull materials, such as glass-fibre, it may be installed on the inside. In this case it may have to be in an oil bath. Whatever installation is adopted it must be well below the waterline even when the boat is well heeled over and remember it is above the bottom of the keel. You therefore have less water under the keel than is indicated and it is as well to measure how much less when the boat is ashore.

Other features available on an echo-sounder include a depth alarm to warn you that you are standing into shallow water and a variable-depth 'window' that warns of both shoaling and deepening water. The deepening water warning can be useful if you are waiting at anchor while the tide rises a certain amount to allow you to cross a bar, for example.

LOGS AND SPEEDOMETERS

Some sort of log to record distance run through the water is required aboard any craft intended for use as a coastal cruiser. It may be a mechanical towing log or an electronic one that is installed through the bottom like an echo-sounder transducer. This type has become very common as it is easy to include a speedometer in the recording unit.

Various types of through-hull unit are available, each of them aiming to provide the most accurate readings possible while also trying to avoid the problem of fouling by weed or other floating objects. The commonest type is a small impeller (like a propeller working in reverse) which either creates a minute electrical current or breaks a magnetic field. Whatever it does is electronically translated into speed and distance run which are displayed on a remote unit placed either by the chart table or in the cockpit or anywhere else it is required. These displays may be by needle on a dial or as a digital readout. Some highly sophisticated units go so far as to magnify the speed so that the crew of a racing boat can tell to a fraction of a knot (or rather decimal place) what effect on the boat's speed their sail trimming is having.

Other types of log unit utilise a paddlewheel, which is less likely to be clogged by weed than an impeller, an electromagnetic pad without moving parts and an 'in hull' (that is internally rather than through-hull mounted) unit working on the doppler principle.

Once installed, a log needs to be checked and calibrated over a measured distance. Thereafter it must be remembered that it only indicates speed and distance *through the water*. That may not be the same as speed and distance over the ground—but you will read plenty about that in navigation books.

Both impeller- and paddlewheel-type units must be retractable for clearing off weed and a simple means of sealing the hole after removal is required.

WIND INSTRUMENTS

One of the spin-offs from yacht racing has been electronic instruments that indicate wind speed and direction. As racing became more and more hotly contended, so there emerged a requirement for more precise information about these matters than could be obtained from a simple burgee and wet finger. When a sail blows out if carried above a certain wind speed you soon understand the need for such information. However, if you are

A fleet of GP14s broad reaching in bright sunshine. Originally designed in 1949 for home construction, these boats are still very popular with over 12,000 having been built. The initials GP stand for General Purpose as the dinghy was intended to be a good general purpose 14ft daysailer and became a good racing boat as well

not a dedicated racing person and do not carry a large wardrobe of headsails I can see little purpose in spending a lot of money on these instruments when a burgee and simple hand-held anemometer will suffice.

For their designed use, wind speed and direction instruments are excellent, don't misunderstand me, but the new boat owner trying to decide where best to spend the little money he has available should think twice before buying them. Don't forget that you can always add them later.

ENGINE INSTRUMENTS

Inboard engines tend to be supplied with an instrument panel which at least includes the ignition switch, an oil-pressure warning light and an ignition light. Some go further and include

105

oil-pressure and water-temperature gauges, while big motor cruisers may have rev counters, oil-temperature gauges, various pressure gauges and engine-hour meters. Outboard motors do not usually come with any instruments, but the boat may well be fitted with the same instruments as an inboard-powered one.

If extra instruments are offered on a motor boat it seems sensible to buy them provided that you will then make proper use of them. This means taking regular readings of each instrument and recording them. In that way a change in temperature, pressure or whatever is immediately noticed and remedial action can be taken before any major mishap occurs.

Another useful instrument is a fuel gauge, for although a sight glass on the fuel tank or even a dipstick will work perfectly well, it is much easier to look at a gauge near the helm to check the level in the tank. You are also likely to do it more often and so are less likely to run out.

By their very nature engine instruments only operate when the engine is running so battery drain need hardly be considered. What must be watched is their proximity to the compass as they can affect it drastically if they are too close. This is usually a problem met on larger motor cruisers where the compass is often sited amongst the instruments on a large panel at the steering console. This is not a good arrangement, as it makes compass adjustment very hard, and it should not be impossible to move the instruments some distance away and yet leave them visible.

RADAR

Radar has become widely used on motor cruisers and large yachts as the scanner units are now of a compact size and low weight compared with earlier giants. They are still large and heavy, but more manageably so. Prices too have fallen to within the reach of a lot of owners and they have quickly discovered how useful an aid a radar set is.

The scanner unit must be mounted as high as possible and be given a clear all-round 'view'—or at least have as few blind spots as possible. This usually means mounting it on a wheelhouse roof or on large yachts somewhere about the crosstrees on the forward side of the mizzenmast. Such a lot of weight so high up puts a deal of extra strain on the rigging and should be discussed with the builders or designer of the boat first. In fact the whole installation of a radar set must be done by experts as they are delicate instruments requiring precise adjustment.

If you do choose to install radar you must take the trouble to learn how to interpret what it displays and accept the fact that it is a navigational aid not a navigational method. Some sailing and motor cruising schools run radar courses and it would be wise to attend one of these. Otherwise a manufacturer's representative may be able to instruct you in the use and adjustment of the set.

RADIO

All boats putting out to sea should carry a radio capable of receiving weather forecasts. This need only be a household transistor radio with the right frequencies, but it is essential to safe boating.

VHF (Very High Frequency) transmitting and receiving radios are becoming more and more widespread as they are available at relatively low cost and provide an excellent means of communicating with other vessels and with shore stations in the event of accident or difficulty, without going to the extreme of letting off flares to summon the rescue services. They work on line of sight, which may give a range of as much as 40–50 miles, and do not require the vast battery capacity of long-range radio telephones.

It is necessary to obtain an operator's licence before using a VHF set and strict radio procedure must be adhered to. If that is done then valuable information can be obtained from Coastguard stations while on passage regarding weather and from port authorities about availability of berths on your approach to harbour. By keeping in touch with the Coastguard you also know that your progress is being followed should trouble occur at any stage of the passage. All in all I feel that a VHF set is a very useful piece of equipment, but it must be used judiciously and properly. It should also be realised that it is by no means essential to safe seagoing, it is just a help.

RADIO DIRECTION FINDERS

After echo-sounders and logs, RDF sets must be amongst the most popular electronic instruments on a boat. Their purpose is to provide the navigator with additional lines of position to help him keep track of the boat's progress. They are not intended as a navigational method, only as an aid.

The principle behind all RDF sets is that they provide a bearing on a transmitting radio beacon or an angle between the beacon and the ship's head. In the first instance the set incorporates its own compass from which the bearing can be read, while in the second type the angle between the RDF aerial and the boat's course is measured. This is then added to or subtracted from the course as read from the steering compass to give the bearing of the beacon. Both systems result in a bearing that can be plotted on a chart as a line of position—a line on which the boat is positioned. Her exact position on the line can be determined in a number of ways, one of which is to obtain a second and if possible a third line of position from two other beacons which cross the first one at a large angle. The boat's position is then the point at which they all cross.

A wide variety of RDF sets is available, including automatic ones which provide the bearing with little effort on the part of the navigator. More commonly, however, the user must tune in to the beacon's frequency, identify it by its Morse code signal and then home-in on it by rotating the set's aerial until the transmitted signal is at it's weakest—the null point. This null can be determined aurally or by meter or by a light, depending on the type of set being used.

Tuning in to the beacon's frequency can be done by rotating the dial or by keying in the frequency and letting the set do the fine tuning. There are all sorts of variations, but essentially, a cheap set is a good introduction and can give perfectly adequate service, but if you want a more sophisticated unit you will have to pay an appropriately higher price. It is not strictly true to say the best instrument is the most expensive, but certainly the more costly instruments are more refined than the cheap ones.

Many RDF sets incorporate a radio which is capable of at least receiving the weather forecasts if nothing else, while some are actually based on a full-range radio. Even though you may carry another radio receiver, it does make sense to choose an RDF set with at least forecast-receiving capability as a back up.

Safety equipment

FIRE EXTINGUISHERS

Fire extinguishers are essential safety items on any boat. A fire at sea is extremely serious as it can ultimately mean your being in the water without support and far from land or help. Even the smallest boat with an engine must carry at least one fire extinguisher, but on a boat with accommodation you should consider two to be an absolute minimum—and I don't mean baby aerosol canisters. These can be very useful for small galley fires, but they should be carried in addition to much larger units of not less than 3lb (1.4 kg) capacity (dry powder). Bigger craft, particularly motor boats, must be equipped with larger extinguishers of at least 5lb (2.3 kg) capacity (dry powder), and may even be fitted with automatic units in their engine compartments which are triggered by any excessive build-up of heat there.

In brackets after each size of extinguisher I have put 'dry powder' as the extinguishing capability of this compound is used as a measure for all other extinguishants such as CO_2 (Carbon dioxide), foam, BCF (bromo-chloro-difluoro-methane) and BTF (bromo-trifluoro-methane). Which of these types is best as a general-purpose boat-fire extinguishant is hard to say. Dry-powder extinguishers are widely used and are obviously very effective, but once set off they cannot be stopped until totally discharged and the powder is hard to clear up after a minor fire such

This 13ft Orkney Dory powered by a 20hp Mercury outboard is used by Jack Holt sailmakers to assist with safety work at dinghy race meetings. A steering consol amidships has single lever engine controls beside it and in common with other dories the Orkney has a layer of foam between the hull and inner moulding to prevent her sinking if swamped or even holed. The cathedral hull form and rectangular shape make her very stable and the hull form also permits planing at quite low speeds with fairly small outboard motors

as a galley flare-up. It is meant to get into every nook and cranny and it certainly does; you go on finding it for months afterwards. A controllable discharge BCF extinguisher, on the other hand, can be used in brief squirts for small fires and the gas disperses readily. It must be remembered, however, that any of the gases used as extinguishants are toxic if allowed to build up in a confined space. Thus, immediately after use the whole boat must be well ventilated.

A sensible practice is to carry several main fire extinguishers plus a fire blanket and a couple of aerosol extinguishers for dealing with such things as minor galley fires. Don't hesitate though to go in with the big fellows if a real fire does start. Any mess or trouble is better than a full-scale fire on board a boat at sea and do ensure that everyone aboard is familiar with the positioning and operation of all fire-fighting appliances.

FOGHORNS

Some sort of foghorn should be carried, whether it is mouth, gas or electrically operated, on any boat with accommodation, ie an estuary cruiser or larger. All inland waterways boats need a horn for signalling at blind bends, tunnels and also at some locks and bridges. A cruiser may also need to use her horn to request the opening of locks and bridges or to signal her manoeuvring intentions in harbour.

The simplest type of horn, with virtually nothing to go wrong, is the 'plate layer's' horn operated orally. It is quite directional and should be pointed at the person you are attempting to signal. In contrast, a horn operated from an attached aerosol canister is almost omni-directional. The main problem with such horns is that the gas tends to freeze on their reeds in fog rendering them useless just when you most need them. Electrically operated horns, usually taken from the car-accessory trade, are fine provided that the electrical circuit can be adequately protected from spray and damp—particularly fog.

LIFEJACKETS

The class rules of most racing dinghies insist that the crew wear lifejackets and water-ski clubs do the same for their members. Otherwise it is usually left to the discretion of a boat's skipper or the individual crew member. A lifejacket for each member of the crew should be carried aboard seagoing craft at all times and it is sensible to provide them for any non-swimmers or poor swimmers on other boats.

It is important when buying lifejackets to distinguish between true lifejackets and buoyancy aids. The former, in essence, will support an unconscious person and turn him face upwards in the water with his nose and mouth clear, while the latter will *assist* a person to stay afloat or swim when they are conscious. Thus life-

111

jackets have much more permanent buoyancy material incorporated in them than do buoyancy aids, which may be inflatable, and so lifejackets are generally rather bulkier. This can be a nuisance on a small boat but the wearer soon gets used to it.

When not in use lifejackets must be stowed where they are readily accessible, not at the bottom of a locker under piles of other gear. When they are being worn, fasten them up properly. If they come off in the water they can't help you.

LIFEHARNESSES

All seagoing boats should carry lifeharnesses on board, but a sailing cruiser or racing boat should carry one for each member of the crew. A new crew should wear the harness on deck in calm weather to accustom themselves to moving and working with the harness on, but thereafter it is sufficient to wear them in rough weather or whenever the need is felt.

The important factors to look for when choosing a harness are simplicity of putting it on without getting it tangled or twisted and security of the fastening. There are some oilskin jackets available with a built-in harness and although they are expensive they do ensure that the harness is always ready for instant use.

One point to watch is that it is not always possible to wear a lifejacket and lifeharness in combination. If you want to wear them together, buy the two as a compatible unit.

LIFEBUOYS

At least two lifebuoys are required on boats with accommodation. Whether these are the common horseshoe shape or the older complete ring is a matter of personal preference and ease of stowage. The rings, assuming adequate size, can be put on by the person in the water, but many horseshoes can only be held onto. Those that can be put on need a short lanyard to close the open end or the wearer may slip out. Horseshoes, however, are generally easier to stow on a small boat.

Whichever type of lifebuoy is chosen they must be stowed in

such a way that they can be thrown overboard in a trice. This means some sort of retaining bracket, without fastenings, placed within reach of anyone in the cockpit, usually the helmsman.

It is also wise to equip each lifebuoy with a light. These floating lights are attached by a line to the buoy and are normally activated by turning them the right way up from their inverted stowage position. They go into the water with the lifebuoy and help both the person in the water and the people left on board to locate the buoy. Most of these lights flash a white light powered by dry cell batteries whose condition should be checked regularly.

Another location aid for both the person in the water and those left on board is a dan buoy. This is a tall, thin pole with a bright orange flag on top, which is kept upright by a weight on the opposite end and a float about a third of the way up. The dan buoy is thrown into the water immediately after the lifebuoy and a drogue attached to it prevents it from drifting away from the lifebuoy. Since the flag is several feet above water level it can be seen far more easily than the lifebuoy which is only inches out of the water. Its real use is in daylight as it is unlit, but at night the dan buoy should not be needed as the lifebuoy light will take its place.

LIFERAFTS

It is now common for cruising and racing boats to carry liferafts packed in either soft valises or glassfibre canisters. They must be large enough to accommodate the whole crew—or else there must be more than one raft—and they must be stowed in such a way that they can be launched immediately.

A liferaft is a surprisingly heavy object to move about and if it is needed in rough weather it will be no easier. Remember too that it may not be the strongest member of the crew that has to face the task of launching it, so choose a stowage place carefully. It is also important to ensure that the raft is protected from damage through being stood on, having things dropped on it or being soaked in seawater too frequently.

It is absolutely vital to have liferafts serviced by authorised service agents annually, otherwise you can never be sure they are going to work if you need them.

There is no requirement for an owner of a boat less than 45ft overall (except for entrants in some offshore races) to buy and carry a liferaft, but if he does not he must give very serious consideration to how his tender can be converted to use as a lifeboat in an emergency. This may involve additional buoyancy and a canopy besides containers of water, food and flares (which will in any case be needed for a liferaft). Liferafts are expensive and are not the complete answer to the problems of abandoning ship, but you must be sure you can provide a solution of comparable practicality if you decide not to carry one.

FLARES

The loose title 'flares' is widely used to cover hand-held flares, distress rockets, smoke signals and other pyrotechnic signalling devices. Seagoing craft need to carry hand-held flares, rockets and smoke signals.

Flares. Small craft should carry at least four red hand-held distress flares and a couple of white flares. The white ones are not distress signals, but are used to indicate the vessel's presence, for example when in close proximity to a ship that does not appear to have sighted her.

Rockets. These consist of hand-held launchers which project a group of red stars, each with its own parachute to slow its descent, to a height of more than 1000 feet (305 metres). They are mainly for use when out of sight of land and other craft. The flares can be used when within sight of assistance, for example after rockets have attracted a rescuer who then needs guidance as to your exact location. A variation on the parachute rocket is a 'Mini Flare' type of device which uses a single launcher for several independent parachute flares, the launcher being reloaded after each use.

Smoke signals. Canisters of orange smoke are used for signal-

114

The Grand Banks 36 is one of a number of so-called 'trawler yachts'. They are rugged, seagoing craft that can be cruised extensively and comfortably as the accommodation is quite luxurious. They are strongly built (all Grand Banks boats are available with a Lloyd's Register Building Certificate) and the GB36 is provided with two steering and control positions: one is undercover in the deckhouse and the other, in use here, is on the open flying bridge. This position is particularly useful when berthing as a clear view can be had all round

ling distress in daylight as the smoke is more easily seen than a hand-held or parachute flare. At least one canister should be carried.

It is most important to stow all pyrotechnics where they are immediately available and it is essential that all crew members know how to use them.

GAS DETECTORS

Gas detectors give audible and visual warning of a dangerous build-up of gases or explosive fumes. They are possibly most useful on motor boats with petrol engines and gas cookers, but on any boat they offer a degree of protection. Do not let them make you careless of normal safety precautions and remember

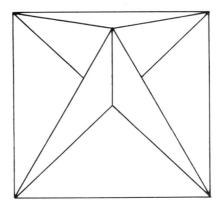

The correct 'catch rain' display attitude for a radar reflector with a 'hole' uppermost. This is the reflector's stable position when put down on a flat surface

that they can fail, so occasionally get down in the bilges before starting an engine or lighting a stove and use your nose—it's a naturally highly efficient gas detector.

RADAR REFLECTORS

The aim of a radar reflector is to provide a strong return signal to the radar scanner of another vessel, thus giving a clear indication of your presence and position. A yacht is basically a bad reflecting target and we have to improve our chances of being seen by displaying a reflector.

Several types of reflector are available, the most widely used (mainly because it is the cheapest) is the octahedral or corner reflector consisting of a set of interlocking aluminium plates arranged to give a number of hollow corners which return an incoming signal powerfully and directly. It is quite efficient if displayed in the right attitude of the 'catch rain' position with a hollow upwards—this position being found by placing the reflector on a flat surface and letting go, whereupon it takes up its natural position, which is the right display attitude. Unfortunately this is not an easy position in which to display the reflector, and on a sailing boat that constantly changes her angle of heel

116

it is virtually impossible to maintain. Even so such a reflector is far better than none at all.

Other types of reflector extend the corner principle by incorporating a multiplicity of corners pointing in all directions to try to provide one (at least) that is in the correct attitude no matter how the boat heels or moves. One completely different type is spherical in shape and by clever construction focuses the incoming signal onto a metal band about its equator which reflects the signal strongly.

Any reflector must be mounted as high as possible, but not less than 10ft (3m) above sea level, to be effective. If an octahedral reflector is chosen it must be as large as possible and the recommendation is for one of not less than 18in measured diagonally through it.

Remember always that a radar reflector can only operate when it is struck by a radar beam. In other words it is passive and can only operate if another vessel is using her radar set. Even then you may not be seen as someone has to be watching the screen when your return signal is received. Always consider it an aid to the problem of being seen, not a solution.

Bilge pumps and bailers

While most racing dinghies are fitted with self-bailers and the majority of yachts have self-draining cockpits, it is still essential to carry hand bailers and on larger boats to install bilge pumps. Where a bailer is carried in a dinghy, tie it in so that it is not lost in the event of swamping or capsize. Electrical, automatic bilge pumps, or ones worked mechanically off the main engine are very useful, but they should always be backed up by large capacity hand-operated ones.

On a boat relying solely on hand-operated pumps it is wise to fit two: one operable from on deck (in the cockpit) with all hatches and lockers closed, and one from down below, again with everything closed up. In this way you are able to inhibit the ingress of further water while pumping out what is already there.

Select pumps of large capacity and lead the intake pipes to the lowest point of the bilges, ensuring that all water will drain to that point. Also cover the ends of the intake pipes with gauze to prevent material from entering and possibly clogging the pump just when it is most needed.

Tenders

Tenders fall into three categories: rigid, inflatable and folding. Rigid tenders are mostly either plywood or glassfibre, but a few are made of other 'plastic' materials. In the 7ft or 8ft size they usually have a pram (flat) bow to increase internal space, while larger ones have a stem. Although rigid tenders are much better boats than inflatables or most folding dinghies to row, sail or use with an outboard, they suffer the major disadvantage for a small cruiser of being very nearly impossible to carry on deck, which means that on passage they must be towed astern. This causes a lot of drag and in a rough following sea they ride up and either try to take great bites out of the parent vessel's stern, or may even attempt to hitch a ride by climbing aboard.

Inflatables at least solve this problem as they are simply deflated and stowed in a locker or partially deflated and carried on deck, usually on the cabin top. In this way they can quickly be blown up and launched when required. Never try to tow an inflatable at sea and only with the bow hauled up to deck-level when in harbour as they flip over on a long painter or in a strong wind and the drag when filled with water will probably tear the painter from its attachment point on the dinghy.

The process of inflating or completely deflating an inflatable on a small boat is either amusing or infuriating according to circumstance and mood, but it is never easy as the dinghy needs to be laid on a flat surface—and there isn't one on a small boat. The other drawbacks to these tenders are the difficulty of handling them in strong winds, either under oars or outboard and their limited size-for-size internal volume compared with a rigid tender. They will carry just as much in terms of weight, but not

118

bulk. It is also a spiritually dampening certainty that if they do not have bottom boards you will get wet feet.

Folding dinghies are somewhat less popular than either rigid or inflatable ones, mainly because they were not highly developed by the time good inflatables came on the market. Since that time not many people have paid a lot of attention to their design. There are a few good ones on the market which combine the stowing advantages of an inflatable with some of the handling and load-carrying characteristics of rigid dinghies, but not many.

No matter what type of tender is chosen it will be a compromise, but it must have good all-round fendering, a strong painter secured as low as possible on the stem or pram bow, built-in buoyancy and it is very desirable to have two rowing positions (one from an amidships thwart for use with a single person in the boat and one in the bows for use with two people). Other features to look for are a strong pad to take an outboard motor and a notch in the transom for sculling with one oar.

6 MAKING THE CHOICE

Once the initial decisions have been made regarding the type of
boat you want—motor cruiser, sailing cruiser, sportsboat, sail-
board or whatever—and the more obviously unsuitable designs
have been ruled out it is time to begin narrowing the field down
to a handful of real possibilities. By mulling over what has been
said in earlier chapters you will have formed some ideas about
your specific requirements with regard to all aspects of the boat,
from her hull shape and accommodation to her safety equipment, and these must now be applied to each possible boat.
When one does not measure up, discard her from your list of
likely designs, until you have a few that come close to the ideal.
Let it be understood, however, that no boat is perfect and some
compromise of your ideals will have to be made if you are ever
going to buy and enjoy a boat, but it only makes sense to look for
one which means as few compromises as possible. If you accept
too many features that you don't like you will soon be exasper-
ated by her and want to sell her.

After narrowing the field down in this way you are ready to
inspect the boats and make objective comparisons. Even if you
are going to buy a secondhand boat eventually, there is no harm
in viewing a new example of each class. You should make it clear
to the builder what you are doing if you approach them directly,
but they are likely to be amenable and can help greatly by telling
you what changes have been made to the design since her first
launching. This makes viewing secondhand boats rather more
profitable as you will have an idea of what the 'new improved'
version is like and can decide whether or not you can live with the

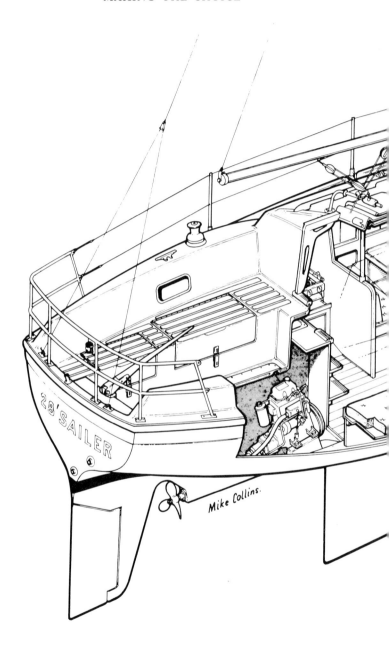

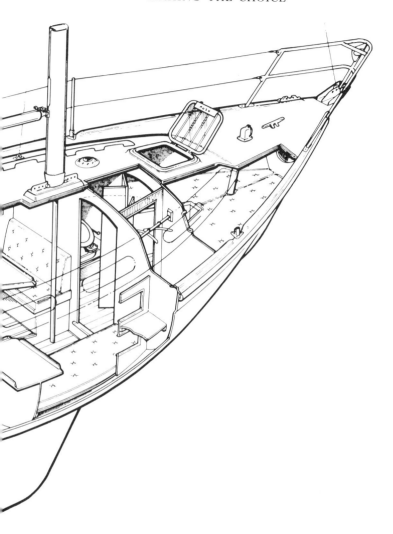

Colvic Craft produces a vast number of bare hull and deck mouldings
specifically intended for home completion by amateur builders. The
designs range from a 19ft motor cruiser to a 50ft sailing cruiser, and
somewhere in between comes this attractive 28ft Family Sailer. She can
accommodate up to six people (including use of the convertible double/
dinette), has a good galley, separate toilet and a chart table at the head of
the quarter berth

earlier arrangement. It may be that the earlier version of the design is actually closer to your requirements, in which case it's so much the better for you.

If you are in the market for a new boat it is both interesting and instructive to accept any offer by the builders to look round their building shops. By doing so you can see the conditions under which the boats are built and will gain some idea of how they are actually put together. Apart from anything else this may stand you in good stead one day if you are faced with some tricky maintenance or repair problem.

When you are thinking of buying a kit boat it is worth enquiring whether the complete boats the builders sell are actually constructed using the kits of parts, particularly woodwork, that are sold to the public. Where this is done you can be fairly certain that everything will fit easily and your job of completing the boat will be that much simpler.

Boat shows are not the best place to have a careful look round one of your short-listed boats as there are always several other people on her, but they are useful for quick comparisons of a number of possible boats since you can move straight on from one to the next. It is also a good time to make initial contact with the company's sales people and discuss with them the possibility of a visit to the boatyard and of having a demonstration sail.

Arranging to view a secondhand boat is a little more difficult because, if you are answering a magazine classified advertisement and dealing directly with the boat's owner, you do not want to waste his time by dragging him down to the boat if you are not seriously interested in his particular boat. Where she is just a convenient example of a class that you think you are interested in it is kinder to the owner, unless he lives locally, to ask whether the boatyard where she is lying has a key to let you look over her. In some ways this is a better plan anyway than having the owner there as you will be able to take a more thorough and leisurely look over her without feeling you are being watched and weighed up all the time.

A broker will probably insist on making the arrangements for you to view a particular boat himself, whether it is with a boat-yard or an owner, since this ensures that the sale cannot be claimed by the owner as a private one which would lose the broker his commission. He may or may not accompany you on your visit to the boat, but he will almost certainly contact you afterwards to enquire what you thought of her. More of the broker's role in Chapter 8.

Before asking an owner if you can visit his boat and inspect her it is worthwhile discussing her in detail, otherwise you might easily make a wasted journey: ask about her age, amount of use and racing successes (both of which matters may give an idea of how hard-worked she has been), gear and equipment (that is the inventory with which she is to be sold), reason for sale and so on. Only if everything still sounds satisfactory after such a discussion should you make an appointment to view the boat, and don't forget when doing so to establish whether the boat is afloat or ashore as this will greatly affect your inspection of her. With dinghies it is not such a problem as it is with a larger boat since they can be launched or brought ashore quickly and easily.

The initial inspection of a secondhand boat

This is intended to establish the degree of your interest in a particular boat by finding out as much as you can about her general condition. You cannot expect to carry out a full survey and in any case that is the province of a professional surveyor, but you can make a good and careful assessment of the boat and her equipment.

If the boat is laid up ashore you can examine her below the waterline for any signs of repairs or obvious damage and if you eventually decide to commission a complete survey you will not be faced with the bill for hauling out and launching which you would were she afloat. Take the opportunity to inspect all underwater metalwork for signs of electrolytic corrosion and, if zinc anodes are fitted, look at how much they have been eaten away and then try to discover from the owner or the yard how old they are. Be suspicious if they are only a season old but are greatly wasted away as this would seem to indicate a serious problem with electrolysis; possibly a fault in the electrical circuitry allowing current to leak.

While enquiring about the age of anodes on a keelboat it is as well to enquire when her keelbolts were last checked and what state they were found to be in. Drawing or X-raying keelbolts is sensible if they have not been done for a few seasons, but is not cheap. The cost, however, must be weighed against the anxiety of not knowing if they are badly wasted. This is one advantage that boats with encapsulated ballast have over those with a bolted-on keel—they don't have keelbolts for their owners to fret about.

An examination of the rudder and its hangings is also appropriate at this point. If there are bearings within the rudder trunk then you won't discover much, but if the rudder is externally hung or has a heel fitting on a skeg, the pintles and gudgeons may be gone over for wear. In an old wooden boat you will also need to check the security of their fastenings, with particular reference to the condition of the wood immediately adjacent to them. This, however, may be better left to a surveyor.

Topsides, rails, decks, fittings, all need to be gone over carefully, particularly for signs of damage or general deterioration. Darkening of wood beneath varnish means that water has got in somehow. Is it through a nearby joint, or has the varnish been allowed to peel off in the past and been put on over damp wood? If it's lifting at all this may be the answer. Will you need to strip it all off, allow the wood to dry out and start again?

Everywhere you go on the boat look for signs of undue wear or deterioration and any general lack of maintenance. Does the boat appear clean and cared for? Does she smell damp and musty? Down below she should still smell sweet even if she has been laid up all winter. Are lockers and sole boards opened and lifted to allow air to circulate? Is there any cracking where bulkheads meet the hull? What condition is the glassfibre gelcoat in generally?

The strength of a laminated stem like this one depends on the proper use of good marine glues. When inspecting a boat with laminated timbers, give them a thorough going over for any signs of delamination. If the work was done well originally and the boat has been cared for since, they should be in perfect condition

Engines usually show how they have been looked after in a fairly obvious manner. Rust, pools of oil, grime and dirt tell a clear story, while a carefully used, well cared for engine tends to be clean (though not spotless) and have an air of rightness about it. If the engine hatch is awkward to get off, tends to stick or requires the removal of half the furniture, it is likely that it has not been opened up as often as it should have been. On the other hand, a hatch that is easy to remove, can be fastened open and reveals an engine space with its own light is one that is used regularly for maintenance rather than for repair. Cans of oil and heaps of oily rags are not a good sign, but there should be a supply of the appropriate oils somewhere, unless they have been taken off the boat.

Similarly, the state of the galley and the head give a good idea of the boat's general treatment. If they are dirty, stained and rusty then think twice about the whole project.

A boat that is laid up won't have her gear on board. This may be stored at the yard, in which case it can be taken out and inspected, or it may be back at the owner's house, in which case consider your feelings about the boat so far before requesting to see it all. If she's pretty doubtful then leave it, but if she seems a distinct possibility, go ahead and ask to see it all.

Where you decide to inspect all the gear, do so thoroughly as much of it will not be looked at by the surveyor unless you brief him (and pay him) to do so. Look at all the seams on the sails, try the piston hanks on the headsail luffs and check that the battens have not chafed holes in the pockets. Go carefully over the rigging, both standing and running. Make sure none of the wire is damaged and that terminals are in good condition. Look over all the spars too for damage and loose or worn fittings. Check that fenders are not punctured and that lifebuoy lights work (if the batteries are still fitted).

You should, at the end of all this, have reached some positive conclusions about the boat, her gear and equipment and you can either discuss terms with the owner or broker or turn the boat down.

Trying the boat out

Whether you are buying a new, a secondhand or even a kit boat it is always useful to be able to try her out before buying. You may have to settle for a sister ship, but it is never easy judging exactly how you will find the handling of a boat by looking at her ashore or in pictures in a brochure.

Most boatbuilders can arrange for you to have a trial either in one of their demonstration boats or in a customer's boat, but unless a secondhand boat is actually in commission it is unlikely you will be able to try her out before agreeing the purchase. All you can hope to do then is find a sister ship and try that one. This is where it may be necessary to go to the builders and ask for a demonstration, explaining that you are actually hoping to buy a secondhand boat, and hope that they have the public relations sense to help you.

There is some difference of opinion about the need to try out a finished version of the boat that you intend fitting out from a bare hull, but to me it seems silly not to take the opportunity if it exists. After all you can only profit by doing so: if it confirms your liking for the boat you will work away on her all the more enthusiastically, while if it turns you against her you will have saved yourself a great deal of time, effort and heartache, to say nothing of money. It also allows you an opportunity to check any worries you may have about layout or positioning of fittings.

A day afloat on a demonstration boat is better than having no sea trials at all, but for cruising boats there is no doubt that it would be far more informative to sleep and live on the boat for a few days. In that way you would have a chance to see how you and your crew fit into the boat and how easy or otherwise you find her to handle. With a racing boat too there is merit in a demonstration sail, but far more could be learned from actually taking part in a race.

For cruising boats a good way of managing more than one day aboard is to charter the kind of boat (or more than one) that you are contemplating buying and taking her for a cruise. Alternatively, and this is more likely for racing boats, you will have to look around your friends and acquaintances to try to find a berth aboard a boat of the class you want.

Whether chartering or crewing for others is the better way of learning about a type of boat is hard to say. On a charter you find your own way of working the boat while as crew for someone else you follow their directions. On the face of it one might think that being on your own was better, but crewing for someone else more experienced than yourself who knows his boat well can be an education in itself. You will also be able to observe tried and presumably tested patterns of handling and working the boat which may save you time and trouble if you eventually buy a sister ship. In the end it is likely to be a case of taking whichever option is open to you.

Magazine reports

Yachting magazines publish a large number of reports each year on boats they have tried out. The depth of study and trial the boats receive varies considerably from magazine to magazine, dictated largely by time, availability of staff and the near impossibility of ever *testing* the boats. To do that would require total control of wind, weather and sea, and at the end of it I doubt whether an objective report could be written as the reporter would either love or hate the boat but would have lost his impartiality. Instead, all that reviewers can do is report on the boat's performance under a given set of conditions (those prevailing at the time of the review) and mentally compare her with all the other boats of that or similar kind they have ever been on. A few measurements can be taken, such as engine noise levels, and the boat may be run over a measured distance to assess her speed (under the prevailing conditions), but that's about it. After that a reviewer must fall back on experience and criticise or praise the boat as he feels able.

Although some club bar gossipers and peeved boatbuilders like to make the assertion that all magazines are controlled by their advertisers it is far from the truth. Any of the big magazines would have gone out of business years ago if they were susceptible to a little arm-twisting and bribery by the advertisers. It is in fact in the advertisers' interest that magazines should be incorruptible because then, if they have a good product, it will receive a good review which the readers will believe and trust.

When you have narrowed the field of your choice down to a few likely boats, write to or phone the appropriate magazine and enquire whether they have published reports on them. If they have they will be willing to send you copies for a small charge, but don't ever ring up and say 'I've read your report on the So-and-so 26 but can you tell me what you *really* think about her?' After much sweat and labour trying to write a fair review of a boat there are few more irritating questions than this one and you are liable to get short shrift from the person on the other end of the phone.

Some builders, if their boat has been favourably reviewed, will often tell a prospective purchaser of the fact and may even have reprints of the review available. If no review is mentioned, ask whether one has been published or not, because however much you may disagree with another person's opinion of a boat once you have tried her out yourself, it will at least provoke thought and may focus your attention on points you have not considered.

'Second Opinion' and 'Another Opinion'

These are two services run respectively by the British magazine *Yachting Monthly* and the American one *Cruising World*. As their titles imply, these schemes enable a prospective buyer to obtain another opinion about boats on his short list, to supplement his own ideas and help him reach a conclusion about their suitability for his purposes.

No magazine can review every boat on the market and these schemes have proved very popular indeed. On one side the owner of a boat registers his name and phone number with the

This Pegasus 700 shows one of the drawbacks of mounting an outboard engine on the stern. Left like this or tilted at an angle, the propeller drags through the water in a seaway and puts a tremendous strain on the mounting bracket. However, it is no easy task in rough water to remove the motor and stow it on board, only to have to reverse the operation when next it is required. Outboard motors have their advantages, but they are perhaps at their best if fitted in a properly designed well magazine while on the other, the person seeking information rings the magazine and asks to be given the names and phone numbers of people on the register who are prepared to talk about the boats he is considering. That's all the magazine does; from then on it's one reader helping another.

By talking with an owner of a particular type of boat who is not trying to sell her to you, you can learn a great deal that no one else will be able to tell you. He has lived aboard during wet weather and dry; he has handled her in a variety of weather and sea conditions; he has modified and added to her. He is in a unique position to answer your questions, and while it's unfair to take up too much of a person's time, most owners like to talk about their boats with someone who is genuinely interested and, in part, that is why the schemes work so well.

Re-sale value

However much you may feel when buying a boat that you won't want to sell her for many years, you would be unwise not to give a little thought to the question of how well she is going to maintain her value as an investment. In recent years, provided that a boat has been reasonably well maintained, she has certainly been an investment, acting in similar fashion to property as a hedge against inflation. Will this state of affairs continue? Who knows? The odds are still very much in favour of your not losing money (apart from running and maintenance costs) by buying and, at some later date, selling a boat, and there is no obvious reason for the situation to change. What is more important to think about is whether a particular boat will hold her value.

If you buy a stock boat of an already popular class and look after her without making any major alterations, you are likely to get your money back. If you buy a one-off racing machine from an unknown designer and she wins every race she enters, you may even profit on the deal when you sell her, but if she loses, you lose. Perhaps the best thing is to be conservative in your choice unless you are prepared to risk a heavy loss.

Lloyd's certificates

Besides their world-famous + 100 Al category, Lloyd's Register of Shipping provides the boatbuilding industry with a whole range of certificates covering building conditions, materials, construction methods and equipment. These are designed to ensure minimum standards and try to assure the buyer of obtaining a seaworthy product. It is still true to say, however, that a poor boat can be built of good materials in good working conditions. Thus a builder saying that his boats are moulded 'under Lloyd's approved conditions' or from 'Lloyd's approved materials' is not saying the same thing as the company that offers a Hull Moulding Release Note or a Hull Construction or Lloyd's Register Building Certificate with each of their boats. The boats of the first firm may be just as good as those of his rivals and he may be saving the expense of bringing in a Lloyd's surveyor to oversee all stages of construction, but you as purchaser, spending a large sum of money, need to be quite sure.

In spite of having to sound this note of caution, I would hasten to say that any kind of Lloyd's classification or certification is worth having as it improves the chances of your obtaining a good boat enormously. It should be noted though that a secondhand boat may have been allowed to deteriorate from her originally excellent condition and so she may not be up to scratch when you come to buy her. That's why you call in a surveyor.

With export sales in mind, a number of boatbuilders are now ensuring that their new boats comply with the standards of construction and fitting required by other European countries. This has undoubtedly raised production and equipment standards in many cases as they have had to comply with the *highest* standard any of the countries calls for, thus exceeding the requirements for other places and benefiting buyers in general. That is a worthwhile gain even if it does put the price of the boat up somewhat.

7 SEA TRIALS

Whatever boat you are thinking of buying and no matter whether she is new or secondhand, it is a tremendous help to be able to try her out before making a final decision. As discussed in the last chapter there are various ways of achieving this: by going out with the owner (if the boat is currently in commission), by using a builder's demonstration boat or through friends or chartering. However you manage it there is much that you can take the opportunity of studying and trying out while on the boat. There will inevitably be much that you miss and more that you would only find out by owning, using over a period of time and maintaining the boat, but any additional information and experience of the boat must help in deciding whether or not she is the one for you.

On deck

A good deck layout with sensible arrangement of equipment and fittings, together with safe, secure working areas are essential features of any seagoing boat. As far as possible the decks must be kept clear of obstructions to allow safe movement without the fear of falling over something every few steps. This shows itself particularly at night when you have to *know* that you are not about to tread on or trip over something, since you are unlikely to be able to see it.

Walk round the decks both when the boat is moored and when

underway, checking the ease of movement all round. On a sailing boat the usual problem area is at the shrouds. Can you walk past easily, or do you have to swing round them (either inside or outside), or is it better to step up onto the coachroof and down again once you are past them? Indeed are the side decks wide enough to be of any real use, or will you have to move fore and aft over the cabin top?

As you move about, consider the location of handholds. Do they come naturally to hand, or do you have to reach for them? You should be able to move quite easily from one to the next, taking a hold on the new one before abandoning the old. Are the coachroof grabrails so designed that you can take a complete grip on them, or are they no more than finger holds? If they are just finger holds you will always have to be extremely careful as you will never be able to rely on them as true fall-preventers.

There should be a good non-slip surface on the deck—or more accurately, a slip-resistant surface. Glassfibre boats are commonly given a diamond-pattern finish to the deck and although this is better than a smooth surface it is not all that good when wet. It is better than decks with a moulded-in 'leather-like' finish and is about equal to ones with a 'wood chip' pattern, although if this is really rough it is better than the diamond surface. Good non-slip surfaces are laid teak, Treadmaster M, She Dek and old-fashioned paint incorporating grit. Treadmaster M is a man-made material laid on the deck and glued down in panels. Its surface is formed into large, well separated, raised diamonds which are not comfortable to sit on for long, but do provide an excellent grip. She Dek is a glassfibre construction, looking just like a wet laid teak deck and providing just about as good a grip. Tissue is laminated into the glassfibre to provide the colour of teak and a very rough synthetic compound is laid in parallel lines like the caulking between teak planks. It is this substance that gives the grip.

Clear space combined with conveniently sited cleats and winches makes sail handling a much easier task. Study the layout of the halyards and their winches to see if you can work them

The Westerly Griffon is one of a large range of boats produced by Westerly Marine Construction whose craft have become the 'standard' family cruiser. At 26ft overall the Griffon manages to provide standing headroom throughout the accommodation which offers five berths, a separate toilet compartment and a practical galley. She is built with three keel options: fin keel, twin bilge keels or a centreplate without something else getting in the way. Will you be able to gather in the headsail as it is lowered without sitting on the anchor, or can you reach the boom from the coachroof to furl the mainsail? If there is a wheelhouse do you have to climb onto its roof, and if so, is that easy? Does it have a non-slip surface? How safely can you get down again?

Then consider the problems of anchoring. If the anchor is stowed in a well it certainly helps by removing one more obstruction from the deck, but can you open the lid of the well when the anchor cable is stretched from stemhead roller to samson-post or mooring cleat? Is the lid hinged or removable? If the latter, then how is it prevented from slipping overboard? Where an anchor well is not used, is the anchor as out of the way as possible? Some boats have a stub bowsprit or a cleverly designed bow roller in which the anchor is stowed, thus keeping the deck clear and leaving it ready for immediate use. Otherwise it is likely to be stowed in deck chocks—are they strong and can the anchor be lashed down securely? Many boats exported from Scandinavia are not fitted with stemhead rollers or any real provision for anchoring—are the importing agents going to make such provisions, or will you have to do it yourself?

Look at the pulpit, pushpit and stanchions to see if they are properly fastened by being bolted through the deck to back-up plates. Consider too how easy it is going to be getting an anchor in or out through the pulpit. Do the rails give a feeling of security, or do they 'give' alarmingly when you lean on them?

While you are moving about the deck, try stepping up and down from the coachroof, into and out of the cockpit, the wheelhouse. Is it easy and safe in each instance? Make sure that hatches are not slippery and that there are no sharp corners on which to hurt yourself.

The cockpit

There must be adequate room in the cockpit of even the smallest boat for the helmsman to do his job of steering without interfering with the sheet-hands' performance of their tasks. It will soon become apparent when you are sailing if this is not so, but consider whether matters would be improved, for example, by fitting a lifting tiller in place of a fixed one.

When you are at the helm, whether it is a tiller or a wheel, think about how easy or difficult it is to brace yourself against the boat's motion, particularly a sudden and unexpected roll. Can you sit with your feet against the opposite sidebench and still see over the cabintop? Is there, or should there be, a foot bracing bar on the cockpit sole?

Thinking of forward vision, can you see ahead when sitting down, or are you going to have to keep bobbing up and down when steering? How about a shorter (fully grown) member of your crew? When standing at the wheel or tiller are you in any danger of being banged on the head by the boom in the event of a gybe?

The helmsman must have a clear view of the steering compass at all times, even with several other people in the cockpit. Where a compass is mounted on the wheel pedestal there is not likely to be a problem, but with it in other positions, particularly recessed in the cabin bulkhead either side of the companionway, it is quite possible for a crewman to obscure it completely.

At some stage of the trials, leave the helm and become a sheet-hand for a time, carrying out a few tacks and checking that it is easy to work the winches. Make sure the handles don't foul the guardrails and that the sheets lead onto the winch barrels cleanly. Can you brace yourself securely against any sudden lurches while winching in? It is all too easy, with both hands occupied, to be thrown off balance—and the consequences might be nasty.

If halyards are led aft to winches on the coachroof, try hoisting and lowering sails a few times to see if all runs smoothly. Consider the siting of cleats in relation to both halyard and sheet winches; the sheet or halyard should lead easily onto the cleat without loss of tension and they should be conveniently placed for turning up the line and later for casting it off. Are stowage places provided for winch handles, or will you have to devise some?

Still looking round the cockpit, examine the drainage system for the foot well and sidebenches/locker lids. The drains for the well must be of large diameter, preferably without any sort of grid over them, for although this may allow debris to get into them, it provides the maximum draining capability. A suitable length of wire may usually be used to clear any trapped debris. There must be seacocks (stop valves) on each of the drain-pipes where it passes out through the hull and these must be readily accessible so they can be closed in the event of damage to a pipe allowing water to flood in.

The locker lids require deep drains round them, sloped down towards the well, so that water will not collect on the lee side when the boat is heeled. The lids themselves must also have adequate fastenings to secure them closed both against thieves and inadvertent opening. The latter can often happen if the tail of a sheet that has been let fly catches on the lid.

On a sailing boat the engine controls—throttle and gear lever—are usually sited near the helm, often on the inboard face of the foot well. If this is the case, make sure that you won't lean on them, brace your foot against them or catch your trousers on them too often. On a glassfibre boat they are best let into a moulded recess which gives them some degree of protection. If they are fitted in some other position, run the same sort of check.

Finally the mainsheet horse. On older boats the cockpit finished some way forward of the transom and there was a short after deck. The main boom was longer than is common today and the mainsheet led from the end of the boom to an iron horse over the tiller on the after deck. Now, with cockpits extending right to the stern and booms considerably shorter, the mainsheet has, of necessity, to come down to some point in the cockpit or at the after end of the coachroof. If it does come down to the coachroof, either from the end of the boom or, more probably, from some point along the boom, it needs to be ahead of the main hatch, otherwise anyone moving through the hatchway is liable

The Profile 33 is a good representative of the semi-displacement type of seaworthy motor cruiser. The accommodation is well appointed and spacious when compared with a similarly sized sailing cruiser. No matter what the boat, if family cruising is to be undertaken, careful consideration must be given to the accommodation as it is all too easy to get on top of one another if cooped up by bad weather for a few days

to be strangled by it. Placing it ahead of the mainhatch keeps the cockpit clear but removes its control from the helmsman which may be all right in a fully crewed boat, but is not so handy in a family cruiser.

Alternative arrangements for the mainsheet are to bring it down to a slider on a track across the bridgedeck or across the foot well at some point. A track across the bridgedeck again removes the sheet from the reach of the helmsman and also obstructs the companionway, but it has the merit of being a strong and simple arrangement. Running the track on a bridge across the well from one sidebench to the other divides the cockpit in two and produces some strengthening problems. The division of the cockpit is acceptable on a largish boat as it keeps the crew out of the

141

helmsman's way and vice versa, but on a smaller boat it may cause more problems than placing it on the bridgedeck. Study the arrangement while you are sailing and see how well it works.

The wheelhouse

In bad weather a wheelhouse provides a welcome shelter for the helmsman and crew, but there are two common problems associated with them. The first applies to both motor boats and motor sailers and is the difficulty of keeping an all-round lookout from the helm. The second is the problem when sailing or motor sailing of keeping an eye on the sails and judging wind direction and strength.

Keeping a lookout from inside a wheelhouse is often difficult because of its structure, which creates blind areas. The helmsman—and I am assuming a one-person watch—must periodically leave the helm and walk about the wheelhouse so that he can look all round the horizon and intervening sea. It might, in a really bad case, be necessary to leave the wheelhouse and look at a certain section from outside. The problem is magnified when manoeuvring at close quarters, such as when berthing. If there is no outside steering position it may be necessary for a crewman to call instructions to the helmsman and clearly this would not be a desirable situation. Any boat on which it was found should be thought about very seriously before being accepted.

The problems with steering a boat from within a wheelhouse when she is either sailing or motor sailing, are that you are cut off from the wind and weather (which is also on many occasions why it is nice to be inside) and it is often difficult to see the sails from the helm. This point can be overcome to a great extent by installing a clear panel in the wheelhouse roof so that the helmsman can look upwards at the mainsail, if not at the headsail. I know of no easy solution to the other problem, since opening doors and windows still gives a false impression of both wind strength and direction. In the end it seems that you must determine wind direction by burgee, tell-tales or instruments, and strength either by instruments or occasional excursions outside. At least you can take the occasion of a sailing trial to determine your own feelings and reactions to these problems and the way they apply to that particular boat.

Perhaps I have simply been unlucky, but I have had several wheelhouse doors fall off during rough passages. Most of them have been of the sliding type on the side of the wheelhouse: the latch opens and the door shoots back tearing out its stop. With that possibility in mind check that the stop is really strong. Also on doors, if there is one between the wheelhouse and an open cockpit aft, there should be a sill beneath it to prevent any water in the cockpit sloshing straight into the wheelhouse and so down into the accommodation.

Sail handling

Working on deck is a time of considerable risk for a crew, especially that of a small boat dancing to a lumpy sea; consequently it is wise to reduce the time required for such matters as setting, handing or reefing sails to a minimum. This means ensuring that whatever systems are employed, they are the simplest, most effective possible, and it is while carrying out sea trials that you have the opportunity to see for yourself how the particular boat you are on is arranged. Is it all satisfactory or does something need improvement?

A lot can be learned by watching the demonstrator or owner set, hand and reef various sails as they are familiar with the boat, so first study what they do and see how it all works. After that, ask to have a go yourself since it is only by doing so that you can decide whether or not the system provided suits you, or if it will have to be (can be?) altered. Exactly how much sail changing can be done will depend on the weather conditions, but you are certain to be able to try out reefing systems—mainsail or headsail—even if you can't set the spinnaker.

While you are working on deck with the sails, be prepared to accept direction and advice from the demonstrator or owner, but at the same time keep asking yourself whether each action is more complicated than it need be. At first it is likely that several things will seem awkward. The second time they may be easier as you become more accustomed to the boat, but if not, note them as factors to weigh up later.

Where the boat is equipped with mainsail roller reefing, can the halyard be eased, the slides taken out of the mast track and the reefing handle all be operated from a reasonably comfortable and secure position, or do you need a third hand to hold on with? If the luff of the sail is not fitted with slides, does the luff rope feed back into the mast groove easily as the sail is re-hoisted? Does the gate in the mast track allow slides to be put in and taken out readily? Will the boom revolve smoothly and does it droop unacceptably when a deep reef is put in? Is there any way of retaining the kicking strap with the mainsail reefed? On a wild run in rough weather this is highly desirable as it stops the boom lifting and possibly gybing unintentionally. If slab reefing is provided, is it quick and easy to operate or would you find it lighter work with a winch for the pennants? If one is already provided, could it be re-sited for easier operation? Having a reefing winch fitted on the underside of the boom may not be as good as leading the pennants down to a winch on deck since the boom can lift and jerk about during reefing, and that could make working the winch very difficult. With it placed on deck you can sit down and work at it while the boom looks after itself. Are the hooks on the boom for the luff cringles well placed and strong? Are the cleats for the pennants also correctly placed and easy to use? Can the bunt of the sail—the loose cloth 'taken out' by reefing—be secured quickly and simply?

If the boat is fitted with a roller-reefing headsail, try setting and furling it a few times to judge how easy it is to operate and watch how well the sail sets at various stages. Should the sheet leads be adjusted as the sail area is changed? Is there provision for doing this, and how easy is it?

When it comes to changing headsails, consider the stowage

place provided. If it is a cockpit locker anyone sitting on that side will have to be moved and the bag will have to be hauled out and taken forward over the deck. Is all that reasonably easy to do? Where the stowage is in the forepeak, can sails be passed up and down through the forehatch without difficulty? Are there securing lugs for the hatch which snag the bags? What about the positioning of the halyard winch: is that convenient for setting up the luff? Did you experience any problems in bending the sail on and hoisting it? If so, why? Is there a simple remedy? Consider these things now, but weigh them all up later when you are not sailing the boat.

The accommodation

Two assessments of the accommodation need to be made: one with the boat at rest, probably in harbour, and the other while she is underway. The different requirements for practical accommodation in harbour and at sea centre around the boat's motion in a seaway, which makes it essential to have a number of well-placed grabrails and posts, fiddles on shelves, leecloths on berths and so forth. It is relatively simple to provide a practical, workable layout when nothing moves, but when the boat is going to be rolling and pitching it is a far harder job.

As discussed earlier with the deck layout, it is during sea trials that you have the best opportunity to judge the accommodation and how well it works on passage. Move about below, checking that there are substantial grabrails and posts just where you need them. An awkward reach for the next one throws you off balance and that leads to bruises more often than not.

When the boat is under power, what is the noise level like down below? Can you hold a conversation reasonably? Is it tolerable for a long period?

In the galley and at the chart table, where you will have to use two hands for working, you need to be able to wedge yourself in securely. Can you? If the cooker is on the lee side and you are cooking, can you avoid being thrown against it if the boat lurches suddenly? A 'crash bar' across the front of it helps to prevent such an accident. Is there somewhere to put down a hot saucepan? Will your navigation instruments slide off the chart table as the boat heels or are there adequate fiddle rails round it? What stowage is provided for them or will you have to make a place?

Going back to the galley, if gas is used for cooking, how is it piped in and where from? The gas locker needs to be vented overboard and the piping must be copper as far as possible, then approved flexible hose. Can you reach and operate the shut-off valve easily?

How many of the berths will really be usable at sea? The two vee berths in the forecabin of a small boat are often untenable because of the boat's lively motion, so it may be necessary to work a 'hot berth' system further aft in the saloon as the watches change on an overnight passage. Will that be possible? Do the saloon berths have leecloths to prevent their occupants rolling out, or will some have to be fitted? Many boats have a dinette in the saloon which converts to a double berth by lowering the table and covering it with a cushion. It works well enough in harbour, though it may be a trifle narrow, but at sea it will have to remain a dinette and be used as a single berth. That means you immediately have one less sea berth than there are harbour berths. Are there still enough? Try out the quarter berth as this is possibly the most comfortable berth on the whole boat, but is useless if there is not enough room to allow you to sleep comfortably, and that means having height at the hips to turn over.

Consider the arrangement in the heads compartment. Is it usable with the boat heeled? Are there any grabrails? Is there room to move in and out of it with oilskins on? When the boat is heeled, can you still dress and undress without bursting out through the door?

For in-harbour use, there needs to be a fair amount of lounging space in which you can entertain friends or just sit in comfort after dinner. Even a small boat benefits by having a table you can eat off properly, but it should not be so complicated that erecting it is more trouble than it's worth. Small boats too will only have

The International Europe is a singlehanded dinghy providing good,
competitive racing. There are some 11,000 Europes throughout the
world, but less than a hundred of them in Britain as yet

sitting headroom, so sitting must be very comfortable and that means having backrests, otherwise the corner of the side deck and cabintop will dig into the back of your neck. On larger boats people expect standing headroom, at least in the saloon if not in the forecabin, but how high is 'standing headroom'? Ample for one person is too little for the next. All you can do is judge for yourself and the tallest member of your normal crew.

Somewhere to hang wet oilskins and leave wet boots is most desirable to prevent the whole accommodation becoming too damp and miserable. On a small boat it is hard to achieve, but on larger ones there should be a suitable place provided.

Ventilation is often rather low on the builder's list of priorities and you may have to increase the number of vents. Note how many there are, where they are, and think about the problem. I don't just mean general through-deck accommodation ventilators, but locker vents as well. Few production boats offer vented lockers and this can lead to damp and musty stowage.

Access to the hull is important. You must be able to reach all skin fittings quickly and other fittings with some panel removing. If a hull and deckhead lining is fitted as screwed-on, suspended panels this is not usually too hard, but if an inner moulding is used it must have access holes (preferably with covers so that you are not forever staring at a series of holes). It is those boats with a lining which is stuck on that provide the real headache since in too many cases it would have to be cut away if you had to get at something like a deck fitting.

Bilge access is also important in order to be able to clear the intake of the bilge pump. Some modern boats are built virtually without bilges, but study the problem and decide whether the builder has solved it satisfactorily or if you will have to improve the arrangement.

Engines

Unless you are a practising marine engineer you are unlikely to be able to judge the boat's engine installation in terms other than those dictated by past experience of having to grovel about working on them. By and large, boat engines are satisfactorily installed so far as safety and proper running are concerned, but more than a few leave a lot to be desired in terms of accessibility even for the most basic periodic maintenance.

There must be reasonable access to the engine from front, back and both sides. You need to be able to check oil levels, battery levels, change oil filters, unblock fuel lines and bleed them. You must be able to change plugs or injectors and check points gaps. If part of the access is provided by lifting the cockpit sole, is the cover watertight? Can the boat still be manoeuvred when it is raised?

Some modern marine engines are very cleverly designed so that the major parts are all reached from one side and this certainly makes life a whole lot easier. Other ones, however, do need to be looked at carefully to see that they can be maintained reasonably easily.

Remote stern-gland greasers save some grovelling beneath the cockpit sole, but you should still be able to reach the gland. Batteries and electrics must be accessible and the batteries must be held down firmly by some sort of securing bar or strap. Ventilation of their compartment is necessary, particularly on boats with big banks of heavy-duty batteries. Fuel-tank vents must also be well placed to allow breathing but prevent the ingress of water.

Filling points for fuel and water must be clearly marked and well separated so that the two cannot be mixed. Their locations must be such that spillage of either does not cause inconvenience or damage; the best place for any spillage being over the side. There should be a water and sludge trap on the fuel tank and it must be reached easily for draining and clearing.

Seacocks must also be well placed and the strainer on the cooling-water inlet must be easy to remove and clean. If the engine has a freshwater cooling system the top-up point must be unobstructed for pouring in water.

Air-cooled engines require large air-intake and outlet vents

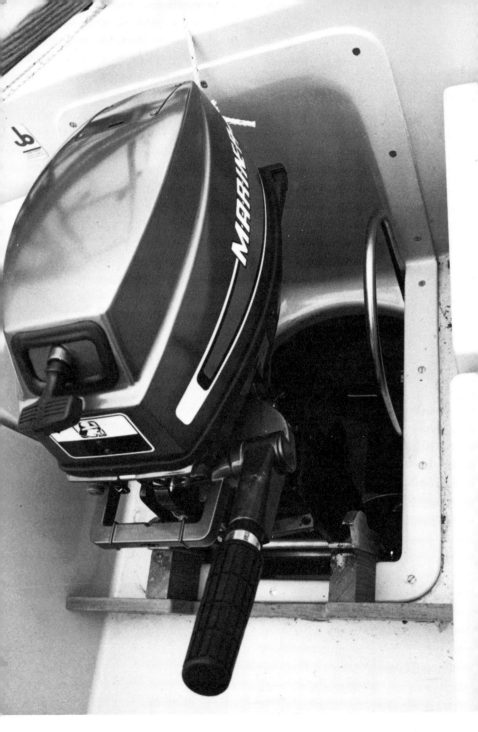

An outboard motor installed in its well on a 26ft Seal cruiser racer. In this raised position, the opening in the bottom of the boat is covered by a panel put in place and held there by the stainless steel hoop on the right of the well. When the engine is required the panel is removed and the engine lowered with proper ducting and room for the air to circulate freely round the engine. Even a water-cooled engine must have adequate 'breathing space'.

How noisy is the engine? Would it be quieter if more sound insulation material were fitted in the engine compartment?

Where an outboard engine is employed its bracket must be strong enough and if it is a lifting or hinging one it must be easy to operate. Consider the problem of lifting the outboard onto and off its bracket while at sea. Do you think you can manage it? Is there a good stowage place for the engine when it is not on its bracket? What about its fuel tank—where does that go? If the outboard is installed in a well, does it have sufficient air when running and can the bottom hatch be closed without difficulty when the engine is raised? Is the surge and slop of water at all likely to flood the bottom of the engine?

Handling under power

Start your power-handling experiments simply so that you become accustomed to the boat. Open the throttle to normal cruising revs, generally about threequarters open, and keep her on a steady course. Take your hands off the helm and watch which way her head swings and how quickly. If it swings to port you have a right-handed propeller; if it goes to starboard the propeller is left-handed. Ideally the head will only swing round slowly, otherwise, if it whips round, the boat is going to be a pig to steer under power.

Once you have got the feel of her like this, check that you are in clear but quiet water and put the helm hard over. Let the boat make a complete circle and try to relate its diameter to the boat's length, then straighten up and put the helm over the other way, again noting the diameter of the circle. Most modern short-keeled yachts and power cruisers will turn like this in about one to one-and-a-half times their own length. A twin-engined boat should be capable of turning extremely tightly if one engine is put ahead and the other astern.

Engine ahead : stern
kicks to starboard
(bow to port)

Engine astern : stern
kicks to port
(bow to starboard)

Right-handed when
going ahead and
viewed from astern

Determining the direction of 'throw' (rotation) of a propeller. Engine
ahead: stern kicks to starboard (bow to port)—right-handed propeller.
Engine astern: stern kicks to port (bow to starboard)—right-handed
propeller. A propeller is said to be right-handed if it revolves in a clock-
wise direction when viewed from astern while running ahead

Next straighten the boat up, steady her on course and allow
her to attain her cruising speed, then pull the throttle back and
put the engine into neutral. Watch how long it takes her to stop,
that is to say, how far she carries her way. Conditions of wind and
sea will affect this, but it is useful knowledge when coming into a
berth or picking up a mooring.

Once the boat has lost way, put her astern and watch how her
stern kicks to one side. It should confirm the diagnosis of which
way the propeller swings that you made when going ahead: kick
to port, right-handed prop; kick to starboard, left-handed. After
the initial kick, try steering straight astern, then try to put her
through a figure of eight. Motor boats, particularly those with
steerable outdrives or outboards, should have no trouble doing
this and modern short-keeled yachts too should be capable of at
least fair manoeuvrability astern, but an older, long-keeled
boat may be almost impossible to steer.

Using the knowledge you have gained of which way the stern
kicks when going ahead and astern, try using very short, sharp
bursts of power (alternately ahead and astern), to see if it helps to
spin the boat round really tightly. This applies more to long-
keeled craft, such as motor sailers, than to fin-and-skeg designs,

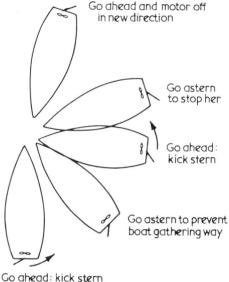

Go ahead and motor off
in new direction

Go astern
to stop her

Go ahead:
kick stern

Go astern to prevent
boat gathering way

Go ahead: kick stern

Turning short round using bursts of ahead and astern power

but it is interesting to try. If you are on a demonstration boat, discuss this manoeuvre with the builder, as some boats require the rudder to be put over in the direction of the turn (going ahead) and left there, while others prefer it to be changed from side to side as you move from ahead to astern and back again. Even if the stern is not kicked significantly by the propeller, using bursts of ahead and astern power will control her position and prevent her gathering way thus reducing the space required to turn.

Finally, lay the boat athwart the wind and see if you can turn her bows up into the wind while going ahead and then again when going astern. This will demonstrate quite clearly the windage of the bows, which is generally far greater than that of the stern, though if the boat has a large wheelhouse it might be instructive afterwards to repeat the exercise by bringing the stern into the wind.

When trying out a sportsboat, something to be attempted with caution until you know the likely outcome is to work her up to a good speed and then put the engine into neutral. The sudden removal of power will drop the boat off the plane and the stern wave will catch up very rapidly. However, it should neither swamp the boat nor the outboard motor, and it is to determine whether it does or not that you need to try the exercise.

Boats for use on inland waterways must be handy and manoeuvreable even at the lowest speed so that they can be steered accurately in and out of locks. The old narrowboats with inboard engines, big rudders and tillers were perfect for this, carrying their way and remaining totally controllable. Modern equivalents should still be good, but small outboard-powered boats without rudders will be difficult to control and in a cross-wind they may prove virtually impossible. Try it, though, and see what you can do, then consider if you will be able to cope or not.

While you are carrying out all these manoeuvres you will be steering and shifting the throttle and gear lever. Is it easy to do both at once? Are the engine controls well placed for the helmsman, or could the position be improved?

Handling under sail

As I said at the beginning of the last section, the important thing initially is to accustom yourself to the boat and get the feel of the helm. To do this, bring the boat onto the wind, have the sheets hardened in and settle both yourself and the boat into a 'groove'. You will quickly find how close she points and how her speed and motion change if you bear away a few degrees or pinch up too much. You will also feel how light or heavy the helm is and how much rudder is required to change her course.

When you think you have got the hang of making her go nicely on that tack, warn the crew to prepare, then put her about onto the other tack. Be careful with a light-displacement, short-keel yacht that you don't spin her right round, as they tend to whip their heads through the wind and keep turning unless opposite rudder is applied quickly.

Boardsailing is spreading at a fantastic rate, owing largely to the low cost of a board and the high degree of excitement obtained from it. The person on the board uses his own body weight and strength to support the mast and trim the sail. Spills are frequent, but board-sailors usually wear wetsuits and lifejackets

Lay her on the new course and settle down again, then, bearing in mind your experience of the last tack, put in another, but this time do it so that her head passes through the wind as slowly as possible. Don't worry if you do it too slowly and she stops in irons with her head to wind; all you have done is given yourself the opportunity of finding out how easy she is to get sailing again by backing the headsail and shifting the rudder while she gathers stern way. Then, as her head pays off, check it with the rudder and sail away. Settle down, smooth out your ruffled feathers and try again. You won't do it too slowly a second time because you have begun to learn how to handle the boat.

After a few more windward legs, bear away onto a close reach followed by a broad reach and see how she goes. Is the helm still reasonably light? In a moderate-to-fresh wind and a quartering sea, this is the time you will have to use a little muscle power on the helm if you are going to have to at all.

On a run it may be possible to use the spinnaker if conditions allow. Only do this though if you intend buying a spinnaker or if she already has one, and watch hawk-eyed to see how the gear is set up and the sail set. Be very careful with your steering under spinnaker but be aware of how easy or difficult she is to control.

At some time during your sea trials lower the mainsail and try tacking, gybing, beating, reaching and running under the headsail alone. Then set the main and drop the headsail before carrying out the same trials. This again will give you an indication of the boat's handiness and the knowledge gained can be useful when entering a harbour or picking up a mooring. A boat with a small mainsail/large headsail arrangement will probably be better under headsail alone, while the reverse design will prefer the main alone. Either boat, though, should be manageable through all the basic manoeuvres under either sail, but allowance may have to be made for a light wind and sloppy sea stopping her, for example, from tacking easily.

People tend to think of heaving to exclusively in association with heavy weather, and although it is useful under such conditions to be able to heave to easily, it is by no means the only time one might want to heave to. To cite just one instance: on a day-long passage, why not heave to and have a meal in peace? The process is to back the headsail, probably by tacking the boat but not the sail, ease the mainsheet and put the helm down. The mainsail, helm position and tightness of the jib sheet will have to be experimented with, but the boat should lie to quietly like this, just making a fraction of headway. Another way of making the boat jill along without quite heaving to is to drop the headsail and ease off the main so that on a reach it is hardly drawing. A well-balanced boat should look after herself like this.

Certainly when on the wind, it should be possible with most boats to balance the sails in such a way that the helm can be left briefly without the boat flying up into the wind. That she does

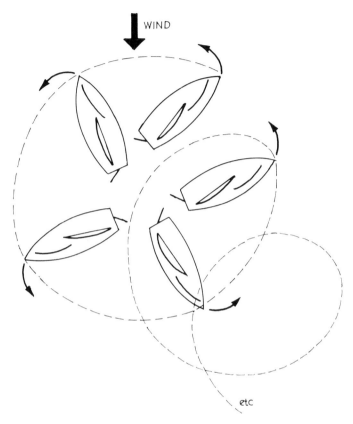

A responsive boat should, unaided, tack and gybe in circles and slowly move down wind

come up into the wind is a good thing since she will then stop, but it should not happen too quickly. Beware of any boat that pays off when the helm is let go.

One final trick to try on the boat, particularly if sailing her in confined waters rather than the open sea, is to bring her up onto the wind and get her going nicely, then tack, leaving the sheets as they are and hold the helm down. If she's a well-mannered boat she will tack, bear away, gybe, come up, tack, bear away and so on several times before running out of steam. In light airs you

157

can only ask her to do this once or twice, but it gives a good idea of her handiness.

If the boat is a 'performance' boat and you are not accustomed to some of the gadgets and appliances fitted, ask the demonstrator or owner to explain their use and to adjust them as he sees fit. I am thinking of backstay tensioners, kicking straps, mainsheet travellers, flattening reefs, that sort of thing. The experienced dinghy racer will be familiar with them, but other people may not and this is the time to find out. Also, allow the owner or demonstrator to choose what sails you use, particularly if the wind is fresh. For the moment, at least, she is his boat and he doesn't want to damage her; he also knows her capabilities better than you do, so take the opportunity, however experienced you are, to sit back and learn.

Even if there is not a lot of wind during the sea trials it is sensible to insist on setting some of the smaller headsails and on reefing the mainsail to see how well everything works. You have every right to show your disappointment and surprise if the demonstration boat is not carrying smaller headsails and if she is not set up for reefing the mainsail. It happens occasionally and does not reflect at all well on the company. Would they have refused to take you out if it had been blowing harder? Does the reefing system perhaps not work? Be fair if there is a good reason, but otherwise ask to be shown how everything works and then have a go yourself to see if you like the system as it stands.

Finally, discuss the boat with the owner or builder. Ask if there is anything he would particularly like to show you: a better way of carrying out some manoeuvre; some facet of handling that is good but that you didn't find. Naturally he will (or should) enthuse about the boat, but there is often something useful to be learned from this discussion. It's also a good time as you return to port to talk about the boat's construction and fitting out.

Taking an expert friend along

If you are inexperienced or want to have the guidance of someone more experienced than yourself, by all means take them along on sea trials, but have a go at everything yourself and try to make your own judgement. Afterwards, discuss everything with your friend and see how your feelings and his match. If they are greatly at odds you must decide whose opinion to accept, but if they agree closely, then you can be well satisfied.

Where there is a difference of opinion you have the difficult problem of deciding how much you value the other person's judgement. Just how experienced is he with that kind of boat? Does he really appreciate your requirements? It's a difficult position to be in, but remember it's your money you are contemplating spending and your life (and probably your family's) that could be at risk, so be sure when you do decide. Perhaps it will be your first decision as a skipper.

8 BUSINESS MATTERS

There is a surprising amount of 'business' to be gone through when either buying or selling a boat. No matter how simple we try to keep the transaction a certain amount of wheeling, dealing and paperwork is inevitable. It spans negotiating a price for a secondhand boat and commissioning a survey on her, through insurance and registration, to transporting a new boat from the builder to her home mooring.

Viewing and surveying

When you go to see a secondhand boat your first task is to have a general look at her and judge whether she will suit you and the kind of boating you are planning to do. If you are hoping to buy a boat that can be put straight into the water with virtually no work needing to be done it will not suit you if the boat you're looking at has peeling paintwork or a rough, scored gelcoat. Such things might not come out in a telephone conversation with the owner, but should soon be apparent when you see the boat.

Assuming that you are not immediately put off the prospective boat, indeed that you are favourably impressed with her on first inspection, you must next go over her, together with as much of her equipment as is available, making a thorough examination. This will probably reveal a few faults, problems or points that you are not happy with. These must be weighed up in your mind as you make the decision either to say 'No thank you' or to begin bargaining with the owner.

Assuming the latter course, you need to make a rough assessment of how much it is going to cost you to put things right on the boat and then make a realistic offer for her 'subject to survey'. This is a most important phrase to which we will return shortly.

Remember that you are going to have to call in a professional surveyor and you are going to have to pay him for his work, so do not negotiate terms for a boat that you are not confident about. If you do that you will either end up with a boat you are not really happy with or you will spend a lot of money having surveys carried out on boats that do not merit one. Also avoid being pressurised by the owner into making a decision to buy. You are on the point of spending a lot of money—your money—so make your mind up in your own time. There just might be 'someone else after her', but unless you are certain there is and quite sure you want the boat, don't let it sway you. To twist a proverb, buy in haste, repent at leisure. With so many standard production boats on the market, if someone else does step in while you are still thinking, it is more than likely that you will find a sister ship somewhere else in comparable condition with much the same gear for about the same price, so don't despair.

'SUBJECT TO SURVEY'

This is the key phrase in the purchase of a secondhand boat. It is your safeguard against being compelled to buy an unsound or unseaworthy craft that you do not want.

Once you have decided that the boat you have inspected is the one you want to buy, you put in your offer to the owner suffixed by that phrase 'subject to survey', meaning exactly what you have decided—you will buy at the agreed figure unless the survey shows up some unsuspected defect which would call for renegotiation of the price or even withdrawal from the contract. Should the survey report show that the boat has, for example, badly corroded hull plating (if she is steel), extensive rot in her ribs and planking (if she is wood), or large areas of osmotic blistering (if she is glassfibre), you might decide that it is too serious for you to go ahead with the purchase, in which case the 'subject to survey' clause of your agreement with the owner allows you to withdraw and reclaim your deposit, or it enables you to negotiate a new, lower, price with the survey report as support.

COMMISSIONING THE SURVEY

It is your duty, in fairness to the owner, to call in a surveyor as soon as possible after agreeing a price for the boat. Actually you will probably be eager to do this anyway as you will be excited about the whole business and want to get it all moving as quickly as you can.

Since you will have to pay the travelling costs of the surveyor it makes sense to find a reliable one as near to the boat as possible. A chat with the people at the yard where the boat is lying, or one near to her mooring, will serve both to introduce yourself as the prospective new owner and should produce the names of one or two local surveyors. In addition, many surveyors advertise their services in a separate section of the classified advertisements in yachting magazines, so a look through there may help.

If the boat is in the hands of a broker he too will be able to supply you with names of surveyors in the district and can also arrange the survey for you if you wish. I would not recommend allowing him to make the arrangements, as you will want to obtain a few quotations from various people and may possibly need to give specific instructions if there is a particular aspect of the boat you want examined.

There is also, in Britain, an association called the Yacht Brokers, Designers and Surveyors Association which can give you a list of their members' names and addresses. The Association is based at Orchard Hill, Farnham Lane, Haslemere, Surrey.

Generally surveyors will examine the hull, deck, accommodation, fittings and such spars and rigging as are available and accessible. Not all, however, will comment on machinery (engine, generator and so on) and its installation, so if you require these things to be examined it is necessary to say so when

162

A Royale Class steel narrowboat. Such craft are modelled on the old working narrowboats. Accommodation is comfortable with all the facilities you could wish for including a full-scale gas stove and oven

you contact the surveyor. Then, if he does not carry out machinery surveys he can tell you and no one's efforts are wasted.

It is usual for a surveyor to carry out a 'general condition survey' which means exactly what it says. If that is all you want, fair enough, but if you are particularly keen for his opinion on some specific aspect it is as well to say so at the outset. He will not be able to advise you on the price of the boat or on what repairs are likely to cost—you have to take the report to a boatyard to find that out—but if requested before the survey is done, he may be able to comment on the boat's suitability for a specific use or purpose. It is also as well to discuss with him the possibility of his finding something *really* badly wrong early in the survey. If he does this he should either stop work on his own initiative, or he should contact you and ask what you want him to do. By that means he may save you paying his full fee besides saving himself unnecessary time and effort.

One thing you may have difficulty co-ordinating is getting the yard to haul the boat out on the same day the surveyor is available. Discuss the problem with the surveyor first, to find out when he can do the work and then go to the yard, fix a date and get straight back onto the surveyor. Alternatively it might be possible to authorise the surveyor to liaise directly with the yard, but you will have to talk that over with him.

THE REPORT

At first sight the surveyor's report on any boat appears if not to damn her utterly, then to cast terrible doubts on her soundness and seaworthiness. In part this is because the surveyor has to cover himself as best he can against a discontented purchaser coming back to him and claiming compensation for his having omitted to mention some fault. With that concern at the back of his mind, the surveyor will pick upon the least detail that does not come up to scratch and recommend major surgery or complete replacement. In principle he is right—a boat's structural integrity (and that includes her fittings and equipment) should be beyond question, but in practice there are allowable tolerances. For example, one worn block need not call for the replacement of every block on the ship, but the surveyor is likely to recommend at least complete overhaul, and renewal as necessary, of all the blocks. In other words, a surveyor's report must be read thoroughly and interpreted carefully. No boat is perfect, nor ever will be, but any boat must be maintained to a safe standard.

When you have recovered from the initial shock of finding that your dream boat is apparently a dangerous wreck, re-read the report and note the main points. If there are some major jobs required, you will have to go to the boatyard and obtain quotations for the work so that when you go back to the owner you have at your fingertips the likely cost of setting things to rights. Armed with that information you can then negotiate a final price for the boat. This usually comes down to a matter of splitting the quoted costs between the present owner and yourself. He may not agree that all the work is needed and then you have a problem, but if it is something serious he is unlikely to argue too much as he knows that any surveyor will raise the same points and he will only be faced with the same argument from the next potential buyer.

One thing that the survey report will probably recommend, if the boat has an external ballast keel, is to have some of the keel-bolts either drawn for inspection or X-rayed. Whichever method you choose this is worth doing for your own peace of mind, but is not necessarily cheap as the cost of drawing them is dependent upon the difficulty of the job and that is only discovered after the work has begun. It is also true to say that the keel-bolts the yard will draw for inspection will be the easy ones, not those, for example, sited beneath the engine. The trouble with that course of action is that the last time the bolts were renewed, it is quite likely that the one or two under the engine were not done as it would have been so awkward. This is one argument in favour of X-raying as all of the bolts can be checked relatively easily. The trouble is that you may have to pay for the X-raying and then pay for them to be drawn for replacement. Whatever you decide though, it is worth having them checked if you intend to go ahead with the purchase and you might even consider making it a part of the condition that you will buy subject to survey including keelbolt inspection. That way if the surveyor does not find too much wrong with the boat he can, on your authority, instruct the yard to draw some bolts while the boat is out of the water. By doing it then and there you are saved the cost of slipping her a second time (assuming the boat is not laid up ashore). Before you have any of the bolts drawn you must be sure you have the current owner's permission. It is also worth pointing out here that should you eventually withdraw from purchasing the boat you remain liable for the cost of returning her to her pre-survey condition.

If, after reading through the report you are uncertain about any points raised in it, contact the surveyor and see if he can give any further explanation or advice. Beyond that, you can talk to the boatyard and seek their opinion or you may be able to go to the boat's designer and question him.

Just two more points: in the original price negotiations with the owner you will have sought a price reduction because of a variety of defects you were able to find and point out to him, but you cannot expect to use these same matters again when agreeing the final price; also, if the survey is really bad or you cannot come to terms with the owner, you must be prepared to cut your losses, pull out of the deal and look for another boat, otherwise you are going to end up with a boat you're not happy with and a lot of bills you can't pay.

Osmosis

Much has been written and more has been rumoured about blistering of glassfibre hulls, an effect commonly known as osmosis or, less pleasantly, 'boatpox'. Nobody quite knows what causes one hull to suffer it and an identical one to avoid it, but the accepted treatment is to remove the gelcoat in the affected area and replace it with a number of coats of epoxy or polyurethane paint. Hence there is a generally held belief that the chances of a boat suffering osmotic blistering are greatly reduced if her bottom is painted on top of the gelcoat before she is ever launched. She would then be antifouled over this coat of paint in the usual way. If you are buying a new boat, therefore, one of the things to consider is the painting of her bottom and, frankly, I think it is something that really should be done. The cost and effort involved are far less than they would be if she began to blister badly.

A recent move to use isopthalic polyester resins for the gelcoat should reduce the chances of blistering as it absorbs less water over a long period than the earlier orthophthalic resins did. Lloyd's now insist on the use of iso gelcoats for any boat they are to give a certificate to.

Insurance

Although boat insurance is not a legal requirement, it makes obvious sense to cover yourself both against loss or damage to the boat and damage to other boats and people, especially the latter. A finance company may insist on insurance before providing you with funds for your purchase and many clubs and classes require you to have insurance, particularly third-party cover. (Incidentally, the insurance company and you are the first and second 'parties'; anyone suffering injury or any boat or other object damaged is the 'third party'.) If you are going to race you will have to take out a policy that expressly provides insurance to the full value of your boat's spars, rigging and sails should they be damaged during a race; otherwise you may find, when making a claim, that they are uninsured or only partly covered as many policies provide for payment of only two-thirds value unless an extra premium is paid.

Although there is nothing to stop you approaching an insurance company directly, it is usually better to go through a broker as he can obtain quotations from several companies and so obtain the best rates and breadth of cover for your particular requirements. This is particularly so if you are seeking insurance for anything out of the ordinary, either an unusual boat or for an unusual voyage. The broker does not charge you for his services as he receives a commission from the company with whom the business is eventually placed, and by going to him you can obtain immediate cover. All it needs is a telephone call during which the broker gives you some quotations, one of which you accept, asking for cover to commence immediately. You are then held covered while a proposal form is despatched to you which you fill in and return with the premium. By missing out the broker you would have to call several insurance companies, obtain quotations from them, then wait while the chosen company sent you a proposal form which you filled in and returned with your money—and that all takes time.

If you are buying an old boat you may find that insurance

companies either will not insure her or that they will insist on seeing a satisfactory survey report. There should be no problem about supplying such a report as you will want one yourself before going ahead with the purchase, as discussed in an earlier section. Finance companies too may request to see the report, and they will certainly insist on proof that the boat is comprehensively insured and that she is so covered throughout the period of their loan agreement.

When discussing premiums with the insurance broker the question of how much 'excess' you are prepared to carry will come up. By agreeing to pay a proportion of each claim you can reduce the premium required substantially. Usually the excess is based on a percentage of the boat's insured value: 0 per cent, 5 per cent, 10 per cent or 15 per cent. It is tempting to opt for the highest figure since this gives the lowest premium, but remember that this amount must be paid by you no matter how large or small the claim, or indeed how frequently you make claims. If the excess you carry is too large it will make claiming a nonsense as it will either exceed the amount you want to claim or will be such a large proportion of it that it is not worth claiming and possibly losing a no-claims bonus (if the particular policy contains such a scheme). It may also happen that you need to make several claims over a short period of time, which means paying out that excess on each occasion, so you must be certain that you could do so without bankrupting yourself.

The other temptation is to undervalue the boat to reduce the premium payable, but this only results in reduced payments being made in the event of a claim, and that, combined with the excess you are having to pay, can leave you heavily out of pocket when you replace or repair whatever was the subject of the claim. Also, in the event of total loss, you would receive far less than you would need to replace the boat. Hence it is wise to value her as accurately as possible and to revalue her annually, erring if anything on the high side. You must not go too much over the top or the insurance company will rightly be suspicious of your motives and either refuse you cover or insist on a professional valuation.

An International 420 class dinghy, like a smaller sister to the 470 (p 81), with her crew out on the trapeze during a winter race. For such 'icicle' or 'frostbite' races crews have to wear wet suits (to keep them warm) as well as their lifejackets

Apart from straightforward insurance providing general cover for a normal period of seven months afloat, five months laid up (for a cruiser), it is possible to insure for gradually increasing value as you build a boat or complete her from a kit. These builders' risks policies make excellent sense, as the boat is clearly not going to be in commission for some time and at the beginning her value is substantially lower than it will be when she is finished. The risks involved during a building project are also rather different: transit damage, craning, fire, boat falling over or a car skidding into her. You will again have to search around for the best cover or, better, go to a broker.

The different facets of marine insurance are legion and each case or situation is different. It is hedged about with centuries-old law and custom, leaving most of us completely in the dark about it all. Consequently there has to be trust on both sides: the insurers have to trust you to provide them with all relevant information and you have to believe that they will keep their side of the bargain in the event of a claim being made. It usually works all right, but if you do not understand all the ins-and-outs it would certainly be wise to seek the help of a broker who can try to explain matters to you as they affect your particular requirements. Make sure though that he specialises in marine insurance.

Yacht brokers

Strictly speaking, a yacht broker is working for the person selling the boat. It is the vendor who commissions the broker to sell his boat and it is he who pays the brokerage fees. On the other hand it is very much in the broker's own interest to help a purchaser as much as he can in his search for the boat best suited to his requirements. By doing so, he gains a satisfied customer on both sides of the bargain—the vendor is happy that his boat has sold, at a price presumably not too far below his hoped-for figure, and the buyer is happy at having found a suitable boat for not too much more than he intended paying.

Having said that the broker primarily works on behalf of the vendor, because it is he who commissions the broker and pays his fees, it is possible as a purchaser if you wish, to employ and pay a broker to act as your agent by finding and negotiating the purchase of a boat for you. Naturally you would have the final say in the purchase and this method of operation would remove much of the drudgery of hunting down a good boat, but it would also remove much of the fun and personal satisfaction, in my opinion. Care must be taken in such an arrangement that you do not pay the broker's fees directly, and again indirectly, by paying a price for the boat which is set to allow for the vendor's paying the brokerage costs. This may come about in the following manner: when a vendor decides to put his boat on a broker's books he expects to have to pay for the broker's services, and so he decides on a likely sale price for the boat and adds to it whatever percentage he will have to pay the broker. Thus it is in fact the purchaser that pays the broker's fees and if you have already agreed to pay them, because you have employed him as your agent, you could pay twice over unless the broker displays commendable honesty by relieving the vendor of the need to pay, allowing him to drop the asking price accordingly.

Many brokers are members of the Yacht Brokers, Designers and Surveyors Association and the Association of British Yacht Agents. Although a non-member may be equally good and perfectly honest, there is a reasonable guarantee of professional standards being operated if you elect to buy your boat through a member of one or other of these bodies. They also lay down a scale of charges for their members which, although fairly high, at least lets you know what you are in for. The YBDSA scale of charges is as follows:

Selling price under £1,000: charge 10 per cent
Selling price £1,000–£5,000: charge 8 per cent
Selling price £5,000–£25,000: charge 8 per cent on first
    £5,000 and 6 per cent on balance
Selling price over £25,000: charge 6 per cent
(All these charges are subject to VAT at the current rate.)

When you approach a broker he will ask you for as close a description as possible of the boat you are after, together with a guide to the price you can afford to pay for her. He will then keep you supplied with details of possible boats as and when they come onto his books. You may be surprised how much some of them differ from your statement about maximum price, but he will regard it as better to send you something not quite right than nothing at all, for then you might get fed up and take your custom elsewhere. He is also only able to send you whatever he is asked to sell, so be fair to him and give him a chance.

Once you receive details of a boat you consider a possibility, you either make arrangements to view her with the yard where she is lying, or contact the broker and ask him to do so. He may or may not suggest going with you to show you over the boat, but in any case, if you decide you want to make a bid for the boat, you will have to do so through him as he will not release the owner's name to you. If he did that you could deal directly with the owner and cut him off from his commission, and he naturally wants to avoid that happening.

The broker acts as the go-between in the negotiations relaying your bidding to the owner and telling you of his reactions. In the end, when a price is agreed, the broker acts as stakeholder by taking your deposit and holding it against the completion of the sale. If the sale falls through he will return it to you, and if the sale goes ahead he will offset it against the agreed price. Eventually you pay the broker the price for the boat, he deducts his commission and settles up with the vendor.

During the transactions the broker can help a lot by arranging surveys for you if you wish, helping you to find finance for the purchase, arranging insurance, obtaining quotations for work that needs to be done on the boat and so forth. He can also arrange such matters as registration, Bills of Sale, transfer of ownership, change of name and much else in the line of dreary paperwork. You may have to pay him for some of his work, but for such things as finance and insurance the companies involved will pay him a commission so that his services here will cost you nothing.

Deposits

In the last section I said that the broker acts as stakeholder by looking after the intending purchaser's deposit against the successful completion of the transaction. That deposit is generally 10 per cent of the agreed purchase price and performs several duties. It shows the prospective purchaser's sincerity; it provides an actual sum of money from which the costs of returning the boat to her former condition can be paid in the event of a survey showing her to be unsatisfactory; it deters the buyer from backing out of the agreement despite a good survey report; and, if it is given to a broker acting as stakeholder, it is safeguarded for

172

the purchaser in case the vendor suddenly decides to break his agreement.

As soon as the purchase is agreed and the deposit given to the broker, he switches from being an agent for the vendor to being a neutral party (stakeholder) and if there is a formal signed agreement he must be described in it as stakeholder not as agent. In the case of a private purchase you must receive a written receipt for the deposit from the vendor which states that it is a returnable deposit to be refunded, minus costs of returning the boat to her original condition, in the event of an unsatisfactory survey report and hence a withdrawal from the agreement to purchase.

Such terms as those above are included in the standard form of contract supplied by the Yacht Brokers, Designers and Surveyors Association to its broker members. This agreement covers all eventualities with regard to the results of the survey being unsatisfactory, the deposits, Bills of Sale, completion of payment, insurance and so on. By using one of these agreements both parties to the transaction know exactly where they stand and it is an agreement well worth copying if you make a private purchase. Indeed an agreement of this type is one very good reason for buying and selling through a YBDSA or ABYA broker. Lists of their members are available from each of these associations: YBDSA, Orchard Hill, Farnham Lane, Haslemere, Surrey; The Secretary, ABYA, 3 Twigs End Close, Sarisbury, Southampton, S03 6EP.

Bills of Sale

When you buy a boat it is essential to check that she is free from debt or you will begin to receive unexpected bills and may even end up with a writ nailed or taped to the boat's mast. Unless agreed otherwise the owner should pay any outstanding yard storage or mooring fees up until the date of completion of sale, together with any other unsettled debts, such as sailmaker's or chandler's bills, and particularly loans, mortgages or hire purchase agreements which must be discharged on sale of the boat.

A Bill of Sale should be signed by the vendor and given to the purchaser to transfer title in the boat and to declare that she is 'free from encumbrance'—in other words there are no outstanding debts. Where there is a marine mortgage outstanding on the boat this will be discharged by the broker before he sends the balance to the vendor but, in the case of a private sale, the purchaser must receive a written undertaking from the vendor that the mortgage will be discharged promptly.

When you are buying a boat and are going to take out a marine mortgage on her you will have to send the mortgage company your share of the purchase price (less the deposit) and they will then make the full payment to the broker or vendor, providing the blank Bill of Sale for completion at the same time. They will also take charge for you of re-registering the boat in your name and various other things which save you a lot of fuss and bother.

Bills of Sale are available from HM Customs and Excise, Forms Office, Kings Beam House, Mark Lane, London EC 3.

Registration

When buying a boat, the main reason for going through the complications of registering her is to obtain a marine mortgage—in other words to raise the money to pay for her. If she is already registered then your problems are greatly reduced for it is then only necessary to have her re-registered in your name with the mortgage being recorded by the Registrar of British Ships at her port of registry. If you are taking out a marine mortgage on an already registered vessel the mortgage company can do all the necessary paperwork for you. They have to charge you the appropriate fees but you are saved a lot of tedious work. If, on the other hand, the boat is unregistered and has had several previous owners, it can be a very difficult job indeed to register her since each previous owner must be traced and various declarations obtained from them. With a very old boat this may be impossible and you may therefore be unable to register her at all.

In the case of a new boat you will first have to apply to the

Registrar of British Ships at your nearest port of registry to obtain the required forms. After that you need a builder's certificate declaring that the boat was built by his company and sold to you; a similar certificate from the engine manufacturer, though if the builder installed the engine he should give you this; the Registrar's approval of your chosen name for the boat which must be unique amongst registered vessels; a certificate of measurement issued by a surveyor appointed by the Royal Yachting Association or Yacht Brokers, Designers and Surveyors Association; a declaration of ownership witnessed by a Commissioner for Oaths. When you have all those documents you send them to the Registrar who issues a Carving Note which gives you the boat's official number and name, both of which have to be inscribed in approved fashion in prescribed places on the boat and inspected by the surveyor who measured the boat (or another appointed by the same people). Once that has been done and the appropriate fees have been paid the Registrar issues a Certificate of British Registry.

The complete procedure including change of ownership is clearly set out in a booklet 'Registration of Yachts G7/77' obtainable from the Royal Yachting Association, Shaftesbury Road, Gillingham, Dorset SP8 4LJ.

Stage payments

No boatbuilder can afford to take an order for a new boat to be built, receive a small deposit and then nothing more until the boat is delivered to the customer. If he tried to do that his cash flow, or rather lack of it, would soon land him in deep financial trouble. It is also possible for a builder to go into liquidation or be declared bankrupt while your boat is being built and unless appropriate clauses are included in the building contract to protect your investment, you may lose your money.

With these problems in mind the Ship and Boat Builders National Federation (SBBNF) has produced a standard Construction Agreement for glassfibre yachts—copies are available

175

from SBBNF, Boating Industry House, Vale Road, Weybridge, Surrey KT13 9NS—and you would be well advised to insist on the use of that agreement or one very closely aligned with it when you commission the building of a boat. It makes provision for each stage of the boat and each item of gear and equipment intended for use in her construction to be assigned to you, so that there is no question of losing what has already been built if the firm does cease trading. Under the agreement you will be required to make various 'stage payments'. There are normally three: 33⅓ per cent of the total price when placing the order to allow for purchasing the initial materials needed for moulding; 33⅓ per cent on completion of mouldings; 33⅓ per cent on completion of the whole boat. Slight variations may include a smaller initial deposit with stage payments at the completion of mouldings, encapsulation of ballast, joining of hull and deck, then the balance on completion.

Some builders insist on the final payment being made prior to delivery of the boat and acceptance trials, which leaves you with no hold over them if they have made a bad job of something. With that in mind it would be as well, if you cannot withhold a percentage of the final payment until after acceptance, to insist on final payment only being made after you have obtained a satisfactory survey report. Doubtless the builder will say it is unnecessary, but it is a simple protection for yourself. It is also necessary to insist on the final payment only being made in exchange for the Builder's Certificate and Engine Manufacturer's Certificate mentioned in the section on registration. There should be no problem about these, but do remember them.

Insurance must also be considered as soon as construction commences, to safeguard against fire or other damage to the boat as she grows. A good broker should be able to give you quotations for this kind of insurance including damage when the boat is being moved or craned.

Finance

There are many ways of paying for a boat whether she is new or secondhand, ranging from a suitcase of bank notes to a five-year loan of some sort. Exactly what kind of loan to seek depends largely on the amount you wish to borrow, the period over which you can repay it and your personal financial circumstances, but the principal schemes are by marine mortgage, hire purchase or personal loan.

A full marine mortgage can only be obtained on a registered boat and it is to get a mortgage that most small craft are registered. Although it does not appear on the Certificate of Registry for the boat, the mortgage is recorded by the Registrar of British Ships at her port of registry and is a loan method liked by finance houses because it gives them precedence over other claimants should the vessel's owner fall into debt and be declared bankrupt.

The majority of marine mortgages are repayable over periods of either three or five years with interest being calculated and paid in one of two ways. In the first plan, capital is repaid in equal monthly instalments while interest is paid quarterly in arrears. It is calculated on the remaining capital at the beginning of the quarter according to a formula of Finance House Base Rate plus about 5 per cent. The finance houses calculate their own rates of interest (known as the Finance House Base Rate) by much magical manipulation each month and as a consequence you never know how much interest you are going to have to pay until the quarterly bill arrives. If the FHBR has risen sharply so will the bill when compared with the previous one, which can be a nasty shock if you have just had to pay for a new headsail or next season's moorings.

In the other kind of mortgage repayment scheme the finance company predicts what FHBR will be throughout the period of the loan and calculates what repayments you will have to make each month for both capital and interest together. This means you know exactly what your monthly outlay will be for the whole

177

period of the loan, which makes things much easier. What you do not know, however, is the precise period of the loan since it will be slightly prolonged if FHBR rises during that time and slightly shortened if it falls, repayments being made until the debt is cleared.

Normally the finance house will require you to provide the first 25 per cent of the purchase price, this payment, less your deposit on the boat, being made *to them*. Only when they are in receipt of your money will they issue their cheque and again it is sent to the vendor or broker and not to you. It is also because they (understandably) mistrust you that they like to do the paperwork involved in transfer of title in the boat, to ensure that the mortgage is duly recorded with the Registrar. It actually saves you a lot of time and trouble.

Whereas with a marine mortgage or a personal loan the boat is immediately your property, under a hire purchase agreement the bank or finance house buys the boat and you hire her from them. She only becomes yours once the total loan plus interest has been repaid, and even then you have to pay a very small purchase price. This naturally does not suit a lot of people and indeed HP is not nearly as common in boating circles as it is for such things as cars or washing machines.

The interest on a personal loan from a finance house is calculated at a flat rate for the entire period of the loan so that you know exactly what your outgoings will be for that period and, unlike the fixed-interest mortgage, you also know exactly how long the period of the loan is. A fixed rate of interest can work for or against you: if interest rates generally rise during the repayment period you pay less than you would have done under a variable interest scheme, but if they fall then you pay rather more. It is a gamble.

In most cases people requiring a relatively small loan seek a fixed-interest personal loan and those requiring one of several thousands of pounds take out a marine mortgage. You would be wise to talk with several finance houses or approach a broker for advice about the most suitable kind of loan for your purposes and

Even after you have chosen a boat your headaches are not over, as the owner of this ferrocement hull found out. It's at moments like this that you are glad to have called in the help of professional boat transporters

about your ability to repay it. There is no sense whatever in bluffing your way into a loan that hangs like a millstone round your neck and turns the boat into a miserable headache. It would be far better to buy a smaller, cheaper boat that requires a smaller, cheaper loan and produces smaller, cheaper running costs and which you will enjoy. That, after all, is what you are buying the boat for—enjoyment.

Getting her home

Unless you are extraordinarily lucky and find the boat you want to buy already lying in your home port, you will inevitably be faced with the problem of moving her from where she is to where you want her. This can be done by yourself or by a firm of professional yacht deliverers.

If the boat involved is small enough to go on a roof rack or to be

179

trailed by the family car, there is not too much of a problem, but if she requires a rather larger trailer and vehicle combination it is best to call in an overland delivery company. Where the boat is a new one, the builders will probably be able to recommend a firm that does a lot of transport work for them and which will be able to quote you a reasonable price. Brokers too should be able to put you in touch with a reputable local firm, but it would be sensible to compare their quotation with those obtained from other companies advertising in the classified sections of various yachting magazines.

Quotations may vary enormously according to what is included or excluded. Insurance, fuel, accommodation, cranage and so on will all add up and if a company includes them initially their quotation will seem much higher than one that leaves them out. It is worth checking too what reduction will be made if the firm can arrange another delivery to coincide with yours, enabling them to travel in both directions with a loaded trailer.

Where a boat is already in commission and can be made ready for sea without too much trouble, it is possibly more economical to have her delivered on her own bottom. This will certainly apply to boats where overland haulage would be a major exercise by virtue of her physical dimensions or weight, but it is unlikely that a delivery firm will agree to move a boat of less than about 25ft by sea because they are then so weather dependent that it becomes completely uneconomical.

Like overland companies, sea delivery firms advertise in the yachting press classified sections. Great care must be taken to select a responsible and reputable company to deliver your boat as there are many people willing to deliver boats who are simply not competent to do so. You would, for example, be very unwise to place your expensive new purchase in the hands of 'couple willing deliver boat UK/Med June expenses only'. By doing so you have only yourself to blame if she is stolen, wrecked or abandoned in some far-flung port. One very good safeguard of professional competency is to ascertain whether or not a firm or individual belongs to the Yacht Delivery Association of 5 West

Street, Abbotsbury, Weymouth, Dorset as its members are all bona fide full-time deliverers of good reputation and practical ability. Members of the Association use a standard contract and comparison of charges is made much easier by it.

Whatever method of delivery you choose, you must check that the boat is adequately insured for the trip as it is likely to be outside the cover of your normal policy.

APPENDIX

COMMON TERMS AND ABBREVIATIONS USED IN CLASSIFIED
BOAT ADVERTISEMENTS

Afrormosia A durable hardwood. Difficult to work as it is cross-grained.

Any survey Owner confident boat is in a sound condition and would pass any survey. It's no guarantee though and you will still have to have the boat surveyed.

Aries Type of wind-operated self-steering gear.

Autohelm Electronic self-steering gear.

Aux Auxiliary engine. Not commonly used in ads today as few boats do not have an engine.

Avon Very popular make of inflatable dinghy used as tenders.

Bm Bermudan rigged.

BS1088 British Standards Institution's minimum construction requirement for marine ply.

Bailer Self-bailer fitted in bottom of racing dinghies.

Bilge keels Twin-ballast keels to allow boat to take ground.

Blake Baby Blake. A marine toilet made by Blakes of Gosport.

c/b Centreboard (wood).

CRE Canadian Rock Elm. A timber used for planking hulls.

c/w Complete with.

C-Flex A form of glassfibre construction employing male moulds instead of female. Mostly used for single boats rather than production ones, and often by amateurs.

Canoe stern Stern pointed like bow.

Carvel Wooden hull with planks fitted edge to edge and the gaps between 'caulked' to close them.

Cascover Trade name of a fabric matrix for expoxy sheathing wood, either hull or decks.

Cathedral Hull shape of small powerboat which looks as though it has three hulls like a squashed trimaran.

Certificate   Certificate of measurement for class racing dinghy, essential if racing intended.

Chute   Tube into which spinnaker is recovered and from which it is set.

Clinker   Wooden hull with each plank overlapping the next one below.

Cold moulded   Hull construction employing glued layers of wood resulting in a light, strong hull. Usually only used for one-off hulls.

Combi trolley   A combined launching trolley and road trailer.

Combo bag   A bag designed to carry the daggerboard, tiller, cordage, blocks and battens for a Laser dinghy.

Current IOR   Has valid offshore racing certificate.

DF   Radio direction finder.

DWL   Designed waterline length which may differ from actual waterline length (LWL).

Deep V   Underwater hull shape of powerboat which looks like a V when viewed bows on.

Dinette   An arrangement of seats and table in main cabin which converts to a double berth.

Dory   A flat, open, outboard-powered runabout.

Double diagonal   Construction method for hull, employing two layers of wood laid diagonally over moulds with outer layer at an angle to inner skin. Generally only found on older craft.

Double ender   Boat with canoe stern.

Drop keel   Like centreplate, but major part of ballast concentrated in the lifting plate.

EC   As in 'lying EC', east coast.

E/S   Echo-sounder.

Electrics   As in 'full electrics', usually meaning batteries, internal and navigation lights plus electric starting and charging on the engine.

Electronics   Instruments such as log, echo-sounder, RDF, etc.

Ferro   Ferrocement hull constructed of concrete strengthened with steel rods and mesh.

Fin   Keel form which is narrow and deep. Well separated from rudder.

Flush deck   Very little in the way of cabin or other superstructure above the decks. Makes working on deck easier.

Flying bridge   A remote steering and control position, usually atop the wheelhouse but sometimes on a tower structure, for motor boats.

Foam sandwich Construction method using a layer of closed-cell foam between skins of glassfibre. Strong and suitable for one-off boat building, often by amateurs.

GRP Glassfibre, though it actually stands for glass-reinforced polyester.

Galv Galvanized, usually as opposed to stainless steel, for example rigging wire.

Gunning Type of wind-operated self-steering gear.

H&C Hot and cold pressurized water system.

Hasler Type of wind-operated self-steering system.

Headfoil A grooved plastic or alloy (aluminium) cover for the forestay (sometimes a replacement for it) which takes the luff of the headsail instead of its being hanked onto a wire stay. Mainly used on racing boats.

Holding tank Tank for containing effluent which is then pumped out at shore-side sites.

IOR IIIa International Offshore Rule Mark IIIa. A measurement and handicapping system for offshore racing.

Inflatable A pump-up dinghy which can be deflated then stowed more easily on passage than a rigid tender.

Inboard/outboard An inboard engine installed to drive a steerable, external drive-leg and propeller.

Iroko An African hardwood of great durability.

Jammers Jamming cleats.

Kevlar Trade name for carbon fibre, used in boat construction and manufacture of some rope.

LOA Length overall, roughly from stem to stern *excluding* bowsprit or bumkin.

l/s Longshaft (outboard engine).

l/trolley Launching trolley.

LWL Load waterline length. Length on the waterline when the boat is fully equipped.

Lavac Popular sea toilet evacuated by vacuum pump.

Legs Detachable supports allowing a single-keeled boat to dry out standing upright on her keel.

Lifting keel Like centreplate, but major portion of ballast concentrated in the lifting plate. Same animal as drop keel.

Log Distance recorder.

Long keel A full-length ballast keel as opposed to a fin. Has rudder hung on after end.

MFV Motor fishing vessel.

m/h rig Masthead rig. Foresail is hoisted to masthead and is usually larger than mainsail.

APPENDIX

MTB   Motor torpedo boat.
MV   Motor vessel.
MY   Motor yacht.
Mahogany on oak   Boat constructed of mahogany planks fastened
to oak frames.
Main   Mainsail.
Marine ply   Plywood formed with special glues to prevent delamina-
tion in marine applications. Often described as being to BS1088.
Marine toilet   A toilet that evacuates overboard.
Navik   Type of wind-operated self-steering gear.
Neco   Type of autopilot.
o/b   Outboard engine.
ono   Or nearest offer. Owner is open to negotiation on asking price.
One-off   Single boat to special design rather than a production boat.
Outdrive   Same as inboard/outboard. Inboard engine connected to
steerable, outboard drive-leg.
Pilot   Any autopilot.
Pine   Occasionally used as abbreviation for pitch pine, but beware as
they are quite different. Pine is a softwood with low durability.
Pinta   Type of autopilot.
Pitch pine   Resinous wood of fair durability.
Porta-Potti   Self-contained but flushing chemical toilet.
Pram   Transom (blunt) bowed dinghy used as tender.
Pramhood   Foldaway fabric shelter over companionway.
Pulpit, pushpit   Rails round bow and stern respectively, connected
on each side of boat by guardrails which are in turn supported at
intervals by stanchions.
QME   Wind-operated self-steering gear made by Quantock Marine
Enterprises.
RDF   Radio Direction Finder.
RT   Radio telephone.
Regd   Registered as a British Ship. This is usually done to obtain a
marine mortgage on the vessel.
r/reefing   Roller reefing.
s/bailer   Self-bailer.
s/d   Self-draining (cockpit).
slp   Sloop rigged.
SL400   Type of marine toilet made by Simpson Lawrence.
SSB   Single side band, a medium frequency radio telephone.
SSDY   Single-screw diesel yacht.
s/s, SS   Depending on context, stainless steel or self-steering.
Saildrive, S-drive   Type of drive unit made by Volvo Penta for use

APPENDIX

on fin-keeled yachts. The engine connects to a drive leg like an out-drive, but passes through the bottom of the boat. Easy to install as it does not require installation and alignment of normal sterngear.

Sandwich Construction method otherwise known as foam sand-wich. Closed-cell foam sandwiched between skins of glassfibre. Occasionally, for decks, foam replaced by balsa wood for a 'balsa sandwich'.

Seafarer Make of echo-sounder.

Seagull Make of outboard engine.

Sea toilet One that is pumped out straight into the water.

Semi-balanced rudder Part of the blade area is ahead of the pivot point to keep loads on the tiller light.

Skeg rudder Associated with fin keels. Rudder is hung on after-end of support bracket built onto hull.

Spade rudder Hangs on its own shaft rather than being attached to skeg or keel. Associated with fin keels. Normally semi-balanced.

Spi Spinnaker.

Sports fisherman Type of powerboat having large cockpit and flying bridge. Developed for big game fishing.

Sprayhood Foldaway fabric shelter over companionway.

Stateroom Marine version of 'master bedroom' with all that that implies.

Strip planked Hull constructed of narrow planks fastened edge to edge producing carvel-like hull that does not require caulking. Often used by amateurs.

Sumlog Make of mechanical speed and distance recorder (log).

Survey Surveyor's report available for inspection.

TSDY Twin-screw diesel yacht.

t/flaps Transom flaps. Outlets for water through stern of planing dinghy.

Teak Highly durable hardwood. Sadly, much that is 'like' teak is described as teak, particularly when used as trim or veneers. If looking at an advertisement for a boat constructed in teak, have the surveyor confirm that it really is teak.

Tender Dinghy, usually pram or inflatable used for carrying crew and belongings between shore and boat.

Triple keel Central ballast keel with twin bilge plates (ie unballasted bilge keels).

vgc Very good condition (according to owner).

VHF Very high frequency radio for short-range communications, either ship-to-ship or ship-to-shore.

VMG Velocity (speed) made good. Usually referring to an electronic boatspeed recorder.

Vane steering   Wind-operated self-steering gear.

WEST   Wood Epoxy Saturation Technique. A trade name for a boat-building system whereby the hull is built using several layers of thin wood veneers saturated with special epoxy resins. Produces very light, strong, durable hulls.

W/house   Wheelhouse. A solid, permanent shelter over the wheel.

Walker   Make of mechanical log.

Well found   Expression little used today meaning well equipped and implying fitness for seagoing.

Z-drive   Make of outdrive unit.

30 × 24 × 9 × 4   Dimensions of boat: LOA (length overall) × LWL (length on the waterline) × beam × draught. If only three dimensions given they will be LOA, beam and draught.

+100A1   A current classification at Lloyd's of London, covering all aspects of hull, machinery and gear.

¾, ⅞, fractional   Description of rig where the forestay terminates at a point some distance below the masthead. With these rigs the foresail is likely to be smaller than the mainsail.

INDEX